Formative Assessment for English Language Arts

A Guide for Middle and High School Teachers

Amy Benjamin

EYE ON EDUCATION

EYE ON EDUCATION
6 DEPOT WAY WEST, SUITE 106
LARCHMONT, NY 10538
(914) 833–0551
(914) 833–0761 fax
www.eyeoneducation.com

Library of Congress Cataloging-in-Publication Data

Benjamin, Amy, 1951-
 Formative assessment for English language arts : a guide for middle and high school teachers / Amy Benjamin.
  p. cm.
 ISBN-13: 978-1-59667-075-4
 1. Language arts (Secondary)--United States--Handbooks, manuals, etc. 2. English teachers--United States--Handbooks, manuals, etc. I. Title.
 LB1631.B384 2008
 428.0071'2--dc22

                                                                    2007048641

10 9 8 7 6 5 4 3 2 1

Also Available from EYE ON EDUCATION

But I'm Not a Reading Teacher:
Strategies for Literacy Instruction in the Content Areas
Amy Benjamin

Writing in the Content Areas, 2nd Edition
Amy Benjamin

Writing Put to the Test:
Teaching for the High-Stakes Essay
Amy Benjamin

Active Literacy Across the Curriculum:
Strategies for Reading, Writing, Speaking, and Listening
Heidi Hayes Jacobs

Literature Circles That Engage
Middle and High School Students
Victor and Marc Moeller

Socratic Seminars and Literature Circles
for Middle and High School English
Victor and Marc Moeller

Building a Culture of Literacy Month-by-Month
Hilarie Davis

Family Reading Night
Darcy J. Hutchins, Marsha D. Greenfield, and Joyce L. Epstein

Literacy From A to Z:
How to Engage Your Students in Learning
Barbara Blackburn

What Great Teachers Do Differently:
14 Things that Matter Most
Todd Whitaker

The Inspirational Teacher
Gary McGuey and Lonnie Moore

Seven Simple Secrets:
What the Best Teachers Know and Do
Annette Breaux and Todd Whitaker

TABLE OF CONTENTS

About the Author

Amy Benjamin is the author of several other books for educators published by Eye on Education: *But I'm Not a Reading Teacher*, *Writing in the Content Areas*, *An English Teacher's Guide to Performance Tasks and Rubrics: Middle School/High School*, *Differentiated Instruction: A Guide for Secondary Teachers*, *Differentiated Instruction: A Guide for Elementary Teachers*, and *Differentiated Instruction Using Technology*. Amy trains teachers in school districts across the country in the myriad of facets of English Language Arts. She is president of the Assembly for the Teaching of English Grammar, whose goal is to educate teachers about current research and to make grammar instruction come alive in the classroom. Amy was a high school and middle school English teacher and literacy coach for more than 30 years. She has been recognized for excellence in teaching by Tufts University, Union College, the New York State English Council, and the State Education Department of New York.

Acknowledgements

I would like to express my appreciation to Karen Bailey, Judy Brunner, David Lee Carlson, R. Daniel Cunningham, Rise Hawley, Jason Simeroth, and Danielle Sullivan. Their thoughtful commentary on this book when it was a work in progress was extremely helpful. I am grateful once again to my publisher, Robert N. Sickles, for encouraging me to create this vision of how English Language Arts teachers can improve their students' performance through better assessment during the learning process.

Part I

Foundations

1

About Formative Assessment

Formative assessment is assessment that is meant to guide both teachers and students toward the next steps in the learning process. Formative assessment differs from summative assessment in that summative assessment has an air of finality. When we think of summative assessments, we think of unit tests, final exams, standardized tests, entrance exams, and the like. Although *any* assessment instrument may be used as formative assessment (to guide learning), those just mentioned are usually used more for ranking and sorting students than for informing them (and their teacher) their learning needs. Thus, the difference between formative and summative assessment depends largely upon how the results of the test or project are *going to be used*.

There's another difference, and that has to do with the attitude that students have toward formative assessment: formative assessment does not result in a grade "that counts." Therefore, students approach it with less anxiety, competitiveness, and defensiveness. The downside is that some students might not do their best on formative assessments, believing that they "don't count." The unfortunate view that students should give a school-time task their best shot only if it will figure into their report card grade is ingrained in our society and works against a more authentic view of what education is really all about.

Formative assessment leads to follow-through; summative assessment ends with a grade. To understand the difference between formative and summative assessment, you need to undergo a paradigm shift in what assessment in school is all about. Traditionally, we think of assessment (testing) as a means of putting "closure" on learning, as though learning is something that should have closure. Figure 1–1 further clarifies the difference between formative and summative assessment.

Earlier, I said that any assessment can be formative assessment. Whether an assessment is formative depends on how the teacher and student are going to use the results. Consider this example: A student takes a traditional spelling test. She gets four words wrong. If this assessment is to be used formatively, the student would be expected not only to learn the misspelled words, but, more

3

Figure 1.1. Formative and Summative Assessments Compared

Formative Assessment	Summative Assessment
Student is aware of the questions throughout the assessment process	Questions on a test are surprises to the student
Timing is flexible	Student must perform within time limits
Teacher's feedback is commentary and/or letter or number grade	Teacher's feedback is a letter or number grade
Evaluation is used to guide future learning	Evaluation is used to rank and sort students
Considers the students zone of proximal development	Does not consider the student as an individual learner
Test or task may be flexible	Test or task is not flexible
Student is involved in self-assessment	Assessment by teacher or outside agency only
Sets reachable targets for future learning	No direct follow-up; when it's over, it's over.
Results are not used as a report card grade	Results figure in to the report card grade

importantly, to employ an effective method for learning them. For example, the misspelled words may conform to a rule that the student needs to learn, or they may fit into a pattern of words that are spelled similarly; they may be exceptions to a rule; they may be learned through a visual or mnemonic. The point is that the traditional spelling test—any traditional test—may be turned into a formative assessment by including a meaningful follow-up component, one that goes beyond mere correction of wrong answers.

Learning should be cumulative. One of the differences between the curriculum and mindset in an English class and one for other subjects such as science and mathematics, is that we often see the study of a work of literature as being "over when it's over": We're done reading *Romeo and Juliet*, so if X number of students failed the unit test, it's over now, and we're moving on to the poetry of Emily Dickinson? But what was the purpose of reading *Romeo and Juliet*? Was it simply to learn the plotline? I hope not, because that would fail to use the many other learning opportunities inherent in *Romeo and Juliet*, learning opportunities that are going to make a student better in understanding all future literature.

All literary experiences offer the opportunity for becoming better readers, sharper observers of literary subtleties. So, the question is: What do the students who did poorly on the *Romeo and Juliet* test tell me about their understanding of literature? How can I use this information to help them be better readers of literary text?

The solution can and should be simple, as we do have to move along with the class more or less intact. But first, we would have needed to know what, beyond the plotline, we wanted students to know and be able to do (knowledge, concepts, and competencies) as a result of reading/hearing/playacting *Romeo and Juliet*. I would propose the following, a list which is not exhaustive, assuming that we are talking about ninth grade students, which is the usual place in the curriculum for our star-crossed lovers:

1. To understand the English language as it was spoken many centuries ago; to understand the changing nature of language;

2. To interpret metaphor; to recognize literary motifs (such as fire and water) and to relate them to the work as a whole;

3. To map dramatic structure in terms of key turning points in a play;

4. To understand how fate, destiny, and unseen forces shape the action of the play; and

5. To understand the interactions between major and minor characters, and how the minor characters affect the plot and themes of the play as a whole.

Aha! Once we've done this, we can design instruction and assessment that is, as we say, *aligned* with learning objectives. Too many times there's misalignment between standards, instruction, and assessment. In English classes, this often happens when we use commercially prepared tests that are available through textbook companies and other providers of classroom resources. It isn't that such tests are poor instruments, it's just that the test makers weren't present when *your students* were learning the literature. Literature tests with short answer questions do tend to test more on memorization of unrelated details than on the concepts and connections that literature offers.

Looking again at the learning outcomes delineated above on *Romeo and Juliet*, let's think about what they would look like as assessments (Fig. 1.2).

**Figure 1.2. Romeo and Juliet:
The 5 Learning Outcomes as Assessments**

	Learning Outcome	Formative Assessment Example
1	To understand the English language as it was spoken many centuries ago; to understand the changing nature of language	Write a modern-day translation of a scene or speech, mindful of the language register that the characters would use (considering age, social standing, situation, audience).
2	To interpret metaphor; to recognize literary motif and to relate a motif to the literary work as a whole	Give two quotations from each act of *Romeo and Juliet* that refer to one of the many recurrent images in the play (fire, water, stars, hands, birds…). Explain how this image (motif) expresses a key idea (theme) of the play.
3	To map dramatic structure in terms of key turning points in a play	Writing complete sentences, express how the events in the story correspond to the Story Map graphic organizer.
4	To understand how fate, destiny, and unseen forces shape the action of the play	On a two-column chart, list 7 significant decisions that various characters make in the play on the left side. On the right side of your chart, explain how each decision proves that Romeo and Juliet are "star-crossed lovers."
5	To understand how the interactions between major and minor characters affect the plot and themes of the play as a whole	1. Identify 5 major and 5 minor characters. 2. Describe interaction between 1 major and 1 minor character. 3. Explain the significance of this interaction to the play as a whole. (Hint: How would the play be different without this interaction?)

You can see how most multiple choice, true/false, matching questions, and the like do not satisfy the learning objectives. So, if these are learning objectives that seem meaningful and useful for further understanding of literature, then you should favor assessments requiring constructed response, rather than objective right-or-wrong answers that test for memorization of plot events.

You may have heard educators speak of assessment *for* learning rather than assessment *of* learning. What this means is that, ideally, students should learn *through* assessment rather than having the assessment be just a way to prove what has already been learned. The process of working through the task that is being assessed causes and forms learning. Performance tasks, project-based learning, and learning through communicating with peers and others are ways in which assessment itself can by the means for learning.

Formative Assessments in Nonschool Settings

Students expect to have their progress evaluated externally: a test score, a report card grade, a written comment on an essay or project, a rubric. Yet, in out-of-school situations, assessments are more wide-ranging. While we do have the job performance reviews written by supervisors in many lines of work, we also have a great deal of self-assessment. We set our own goals, timelines, indicators of how we have fared and what we need to do. In nonwork situations, we may have various channels through which to judge the quality of our work or play. But, whether at work or at play, we still self-assess against our own goals.

Much of the frustration of both teachers and students arises from the artificiality of school; and so, we try to make content and assessment as authentic as possible. Traditional tests are inauthentic, hit-and-miss ways of assessing knowledge and skills: There's no way to know what the test taker does know and can do that was related to the subject but happened to *not* be asked on the test. The high-stakes nature of *any* test can create anxiety, which impedes a true reading of the test-taker's knowledge and skill. Who hasn't underperformed because of anxiety under test-like conditions?

With apologies to Robert Frost, "something there is that doesn't love a test." The idea behind authentic formative assessment is to allow teachers and students to access information about the students' progress in response to intervention without there being a test "that counts." Formative assessments create a working relationship, not an adversarial relationship between teachers and students.

Responses to Formative Assessments

Teachers can use the results of formative assessments to adjust their teaching strategies and to match students with appropriate materials and learning conditions. Formative assessment information can determine:

- How to group students
- Whether students need alternative materials
- Whether students are ready to advance
- The amount of time to be allocated to a particular learning experience, such as reading and understanding *The Scarlet Letter*
- Whether students are understanding a poem's literal level, before moving on to its interpretative possibilities
- What concepts may need to be retaught to the entire class, or to certain students

If a teacher does not intend to regroup, reteach, scaffold, or change any learning conditions as a result of formative assessment information, then there's no point in doing any formative assessment. Therefore, teachers using formative assessment need an array of alternatives (methods and materials). If the goal is to *cover, get through, finish up,* putting every student through the same paces at the same rate with the same resources, then formative assessment does not achieve its purpose. Formative assessments must be responded to by intervention by both teacher and student: which means, the administration must supply needed resources.

Formative Assessments and Pretests: What's the Difference?

Mrs. White is a seventh grade teacher who gives spelling pretests on Mondays. The students correct their own tests. For homework, students are to do the exercises in the spelling workbook (mostly filling in blanks). They take the spelling test on Fridays and move on to a new list on Monday. Mrs. White thinks her program is working because students do spell words correctly on Friday that they got wrong on Monday. Parents approve of Mrs. White's manner of teaching spelling because it is how they "learned" spelling when they went to school, and because the spelling list and routine give them a way that they can "help" their children at home. In fact, most of the parents do nothing more than just drill the spelling words. And, in fact, there's a lack of transfer between the words spelled correctly on the Friday test and the actual use of those same words in the students' writing. It's a mystery.

For Mrs. White's spelling pretest to actually be formative assessment, she would have to, first of all, be aware of the particular spelling patterns and rules that characterize the words in each weekly list. Then, she would have to treat the pretests as informative data about how her spelling instruction should go.

Summary

Formative assessment is a means of communication between teacher and student, guiding the teacher toward appropriate instructional decisions and providing encouraging feedback to the student. You've probably been using all kinds of formative assessments without realizing that they were called, which is something that often happens in education and communication. But when we give a name to something, such as formative assessment, we can transform what we are doing *intuitively* into an *intentional* practice. Our awareness of formative assessment will make us better communicators and planners.

2
English Language Arts Standards and Assessment

Chapter Overview

This chapter will tell you what you need to know about the English Language Arts Standards with regard to formative assessment.

- ♦ What is the theory behind the Standards?
- ♦ What are the Standards for English Language Arts?
- ♦ What are the instructional implications of the Standards?
- ♦ NCTE/IRA Standards phrased as questions

What Is the Theory Behind the Standards?

The term *standards* when used in an educational context, refers to a list of statements that describe the concepts and competencies that students should have in their grasp at the end of their schooling. We capitalize *Standards* when we are referring to a designated list, whether that be the list of Standards set forth by a state education department, or the list that comes from the National Council of Teachers of English/International Reading Association (NCTE/IRA). In this book, the Standards are a distillation of both, expressed in accessible language.

We want students to have certain knowledge and skills by the time they receive their diplomas. Standards, then, are learning outcomes. We speak of "standards" and "benchmarks." The difference between a Standard and a benchmark is the difference between commencement (graduation) objectives and interim (grade-level) objectives. The Standard represents the overall destination; the benchmarks are stops (checkpoints) along the way.

In New Jersey, for example, the English Language Arts Standards assert four basic assumptions:

1. Language use is an active process of constructing meaning.
2. Language develops in a social context.
3. Language ability increases in complexity if language is used in increasingly complex ways.
4. Learners achieve language arts literacy not by adding skills one-by-one to their repertoire, but rather by using and exploring language in its many dimensions.

The standards, or learning goals, for English Language Arts are usually presented as a list of discrete skills, but these skills are overlapping and interdependent. We need to regard the standards as a whole. They are about instilling an educated approach to language, rather than "covering" a set body of material. Teaching the standards means teaching higher order thinking: making judgments, evaluating information, developing a broad language repertoire, becoming an efficient and careful reader, distinguishing the nuances of language, adjusting one's communication style to the situation and audience. The standards have to do with habits of mind: considering the perspective of a writer, looking for multiple meanings, having a willingness to reread, being able to adjust one's reading rate, knowing what to expect from a particular genre.

What Are the Standards for English Language Arts?

As you might expect, the Standards are not uniform in language across state lines. They vary in layout and terminology. What is called "Cumulative Progress Indicators" in one state may be called "Benchmarks" in another, "Performance Indicators" in another, "Standards of Learning" in another. One state refers to "credibility" in the same context that another refers to "perspective." In New York, one of the Standards under the "literary response and expression" category states: "…evaluate literary merit based on an understanding of the genre and the literary elements." In New Jersey, a corresponding Standard is worded as "…understand the study of literature and theories of literary criticism." Within states, and even within districts, what is referred to as "linked passages" is called "comparative literature" somewhere else, and "controlling idea" somewhere else.

The closest we come to having national standards is the list set forth by the NCTE/IRA (National Council of Teachers of English/International Reading Association):

1. Students *read a wide range of print and nonprint texts* to build an understanding of texts, of themselves, and of the cultures of the United States and the world; to acquire new information; to respond to the needs and demands of society and the workplace; and for personal fulfillment. Among these texts are fiction and nonfiction, classic and contemporary works.

2. Students read a *wide range of literature from many periods and in many genres* to build an understanding of the many dimensions (e.g., philosophical, ethical, aesthetic) of human experience.

3. Students *apply a wide range of strategies to comprehend, interpret, evaluate, and appreciate texts*. They draw on their prior experience, their interactions with other readers and writers, their knowledge of word meaning and other texts, their word identification strategies, and their understanding of textual features (e.g., sound–letter correspondence, sentence structure, context, graphics).

4. Students *adjust their use of spoken, written, and visual language* (e.g., conventions, style, vocabulary) to communicate effectively with a variety of audiences and for different purposes.

5. Students employ a wide range of strategies as they write and use *different writing process elements* appropriately to communicate with *different audiences for a variety of purposes*.

6. Students *apply knowledge of language structure, language conventions* (e.g., spelling and punctuation), media techniques, figurative language and genre to create, critique, and discuss print and nonprint texts.

7. Students *conduct research* on issues and interests by generating ideas and questions, and by posing problems. They gather, evaluate, and synthesize data from a variety of sources (e.g., print and nonprint texts, artifacts, people) to communicate their discoveries in ways that suit their purpose and audience.

8. Students use a *variety of technological and informational resources* (e.g., libraries, databases, computer networks, video) to gather and synthesize information and to create and communicate knowledge.

9. Students develop an understanding of and respect for *diversity in language use*, patterns, and dialects across cultures, ethnic groups, geographic regions, and social roles.

10. *Students whose first language is not English make use of their first language to develop competency in the English language* and to develop understanding of content across the curriculum.

11. Students participate as knowledgeable, reflective, creative, and critical members of a *variety of literacy communities*.

The following chart presents standards in accessible, vernacular language on the left side. The right side lists some types of performance tasks that correspond to these standards.

Standards in Accessible Language	Standard
1. Learn to use word analysis and vocabulary-building techniques.	♦ Analyze contextual cues ♦ Present "word stories" the etymological history of a word ♦ Find synonyms and perceive distinctions between them ♦ See the relationship between words in English and words in other Latinate languages ♦ Organize word lists according to roots, prefixes, suffixes ♦ Keep a personal word journal ♦ Use and understand idioms, literal/figurative language, denotation and connotation ♦ Play word games; do crossword puzzles
2. Apply reading strategies, including both literal and inferential comprehension skills, to improve understanding of written works.	♦ Take notes, summarize, paraphrase, outline ♦ Extract salient information from the text ♦ Perceive multiple levels of meaning ♦ Be able to skim, scan, and review reading material ♦ Read a variety of texts for a variety of purposes ♦ Adjust reading rate to suit the text and purpose ♦ Keep a reader response journal ♦ Participate in a literary discussion group
3. Use headings, captions, pictures, and other textual clues to enhance understanding.	♦ Use scanning techniques to get a gist of reading material before reading ♦ Develop the habit of reading editor's notes, side notes, footnotes, captions ♦ Pay attention to graphics to enhance and clarify meaning

Standards in Accessible Language	Standard
4. Interpret tables, graphs, charts, maps.	♦ Incorporate tables, graphs, charts, maps in their own writing ♦ Translate such information into their own words ♦ Develop the habit of reading both the text and the graphic information
5. Identify the distinct qualities of literary genres.	♦ Write original pieces in various genres ♦ Predict the features of a piece which is presented as a particular genre ♦ Read a variety of genres ♦ Translate literature from one genre to another ♦ Compile thematic anthologies consisting of various genres ♦ Write and/or recognize parodies of particular genres
6. Identify the distinct qualities of subgenres.	♦ List and identify subgenres of a particular genre, e.g., types of mystery stories: *the detective story, the whodunit, the gothic mystery*, etc. ♦ Identify the distinguishing characteristics and nuances of a subgenre
7. Understand how literary elements and techniques convey meaning and add nuance and beauty to a written work.	♦ Write original pieces, using literary techniques ♦ Distinguish between figurative and literal language ♦ Read a wide variety of works of literary merit ♦ Identify poetic elements in prose as well as poetry ♦ Distinguish between literary and non literary writing
8. Understand and use the terminology of literary criticism.	♦ Read reviews of books, film, art, and music, noting the features of this genre ♦ Establish criteria for judging a work of literature ♦ Justify one's opinion about the quality of a work of literature

Standards in Accessible Language	**Standard**
9. Read and understand literature of various cultures and eras.	♦ Compile anthologies of multicultural literature on a particular theme ♦ Discern aspects of life which are universal to all cultures ♦ Discern aspects of life which are indigenous to specific cultures ♦ Develop interdisciplinary awareness of the links between English and social studies ♦ Read complete works as well as abridgments, excerpts, adaptations and film versions of literary classics
10. Research skills: Identify, organize, analyze, and use information from various sources.	♦ Write various types of research papers ♦ Write reports and feature articles ♦ Paraphrase, giving credit to the source ♦ Compose a formal bibliography or list of works cited ♦ Use modern documentation techniques ♦ Compile annotated bibliographies on a particular subject ♦ Solve problems, using research from various sources ♦ Have library scavenger hunts
11. Write for a variety of purposes and audiences.	♦ Express the same message in different ways, for different audiences ♦ Write for real audiences, outside of school: *letters to the editor, proposals, petitions, memos, letters to authors, etc.* ♦ Adjust tone and point of view to suit the audience and situation

Standards in Accessible Language	Standard
12. Use the writing process effectively.	◆ Use prewriting strategies
	◆ Understand that time management skills are part of the writing process
	◆ Use editing and peer review strategies
	◆ Use revision strategies effectively
	◆ Share one's writing with others
	◆ Respond to the writing of others
	◆ Support interpretations, decisions, assertions
	◆ Use a variety of organizational patterns
	◆ Use proofreading skills effectively
13. Write in a variety of genres.	◆ Express versions of the same idea in the form of several genres
	◆ Write parodies
	◆ Write in the nonfiction genres: business reports, advertising, reviews, sportswriting, etc.
	◆ Write sequels, prequels, and "lost chapters" mimicking the style of the author.
14. Understand and apply the concept of voice.	◆ Write personal journals in one's own voice
	◆ Write personal journals, adopting the voice of fictitious or historical characters
	◆ Read and write humorous monologues
15. Understand and apply the concept of tone.	◆ Recognize, read and write satire
	◆ Distinguish between denotation and connotation
	◆ Express the same message in different tones
16. Understand the importance of sensory detail in a written work.	◆ Identify sensory detail in literature
	◆ Write descriptions that are rich in sensory detail
	◆ Identify sensory detail in sportswriting and music reviews

Standards in Accessible Language	**Standard**
17. Use correct grammar, spelling, punctuation, capitalization, and structure.	♦ Proofread and edit own drafts ♦ Proofread and edit drafts written by others ♦ Develop a personal spelling demons list ♦ Distinguish between active and passive voice and use these styles effectively ♦ Assist in the development of a schoolwide stylesheet ♦ Develop the habit of using a reference guide
18. Listen effectively in a variety of situations.	♦ Know and use one's own best listening comprehension strategies ♦ Participate in formal interviews ♦ Practice effective listening habits: eye contact, note taking, asking questions, etc. ♦ Develop strategies to screen out distractions ♦ Develop strategies to focus on key concepts
19. Speak effectively in a variety of situations.	♦ Participate in formal interviews, panel discussions, planned and extemporaneous presentations of various lengths ♦ View and critique oneself on videotape ♦ Interpret body language cues ♦ Develop both a formal and an informal style of speech
20. Use effective viewing strategies for nonprint media.	♦ Understand the relationship between graphic and text ♦ Interpret overt and subtle visual symbols ♦ Recognize foreshadowing in film ♦ Develop cultural literacy in the world of film: understand why certain films have landmark significance; identify hallmark scenes, know the significant contributions of various directors

What Are the Instructional Implications of the Standards?

When we put the Standards into plain English, we can see that the goal is to have students engage in higher-level thinking that will serve them across the disciplines. The Standards require active learning with plenty of communication among peers. The Standards are not achieved through teacher talk, but through an atmosphere that promotes student talk. The teacher's role is not merely to disseminate information and evaluate performance, but to foster, model, and preside over a rich and complex learning environment.

Also clear is the contextual, overlapping, and recursive nature of the Standards. Once we've completed a performance task that focuses on a particular Standard, we don't then just make a checkmark and consider that Standard "done." Nor do we divvy up the list of Standards and say, "Ninth grade does the first five, tenth grade does six through ten, etc."

The Standards are designed K–12 and, in many ways, represent more of a philosophy than a prescription, which is probably how they differ from "behavioral objectives." They are not finite, and that is how they differ from "basic competencies."

Many of the Standards are more about the *how* of learning, than about the *what*: they represent thinking strategies, rather than a body of knowledge. They allow for individual learning styles and invite reflection.

The formative assessments in this book that deal with poetry, for example, don't focus on the content of particular poems. Rather, they teach students how to "unwrap" any poem, how to use prior knowledge to approach complex language.

The Standards are a lens through which we view the wide scope of English Language Arts instruction. Language is our most complex achievement. Assessing competencies in anything so broad demands a variety of formative assessments. Some, such as research papers and portfolios, span weeks or months. Others, such as in-class essays, take one period to complete. Some Standards, by their very nature, cannot be accomplished by the individual alone, but must be accomplished through communication with others. The Standards promote communication outside the classroom, with people of different generations, among people of different cultures.

What Role Does Grammar Instruction Play in the Standards?

In this book, the terms *grammar* and *syntax* are used interchangeably. At the outset, we will establish the distinction between *grammar/syntax* and *usage* (aka *mechanics, conventions*). By grammar, we refer to the understanding of the language of the language. Students need to know what the following instruction means:

> Sharpen your focus by getting more specific with your nouns. Eliminate superfluous modifiers. Vary your sentence structure by beginning some sentences with prepositional phrases instead of with the subject. Your writing will be more interesting and complex if you incorporate more subordinate clauses, but don't allow a subordinate clause to stand as a complete sentence.

Simply put, we can't speak coherently about language unless we have the terminology. To the extent that having an understanding of grammatical concepts allows us to communicate about language, we need to understand certain concepts. These concepts should be embedded in performance tasks: Students should have a way of *using* what they learn about grammar. Thus, grammar instruction is a means to an end and the end is clear, concise, interesting, appropriate language.

Various terms refer to the set of dos and don'ts in Standard English. *Conventions, usage,* and *mechanics* are the terms we use to denote the rules. We know that such matters are best taught in context, rather than as isolated skills.

Even the most casual discussion of grammar engages us in a confusing array of nomenclature. Half the frustration of teaching (and learning) grammar is that someone is always laying on new names for a concept that already had a confusing name: a participial adjective is now being called a gerundive; a main clause may be called a dependent clause. Adding to that frustration is the fact that many English teachers, untrained as grammarians, shy away from grammar instruction altogether, thinking that "the writing process" takes care of it all.

Knowing that the world will never speak a unified language of grammar, we can try to have an agreed-upon lexicon in-house, but there's not much we can do about the fact that grammarians, linguists, and editors simply have different terms for the same things. What's a comma splice to one is called a run-on to another, a comma blunder to another, and a fused sentence to still another. There's not much we can do about that except to consider it part of the wonderful profusion of words that populate the English language.

That said, grammar instruction, whether it be prescriptive (dos and don'ts) or rhetorical (knowing the language of the language), should undergird the Standards. What, then, should students know and be able to do in terms of grammar? The Assembly of Teachers of English Grammar (ATEG), an affiliate of the National Council of Teachers of English, is in the process of writing Standards for grammar instruction. Realize that these Standards should not be taught separately, but integrated into the other Standards:

...that students will...

Speak and write comfortably in Standard English, with an awareness of the appropriateness of dialect and nonstandard idiom in some situations.

Be conversant in the grammatical structure of a text and show knowledge of the relationship between meaning and grammar, and how changes in one effect changes in the other.

Understand that language changes across time, from region to region, and in various social situations. Students will appreciate and value linguistic variations and will understand the nature of dialect-based prejudices.

Appreciate the fact that cultural variations and dialect contribute to our nation's heritage and are to be valued in terms of expressive capacity, logical structure, and beauty.

Our job as English teachers is to make students secure in their use of Standard English. Lack of education in the vagaries of Standard English renders a speaker/writer insecure. The secure speaker/writer is able to recognize when Standard English prescriptives are inappropriate to the context.

There is a subtle but significant distinction among the terms *objectives, competencies,* and *standards.* Standards are expressed differently by different states and bureaus, but, once we put them into plain English, we can develop performance tasks to assess them and we can see how they are the guiding lights of instruction. The Standards are presented in the form of a numbered list, as if they are discrete skills to be mastered one at a time. But they are in fact highly interconnected and achieved cumulatively, over the course of many years.

Here are the NCTE/IRA Standards phrased as questions:

- ◆ Can you analyze, interpret, evaluate what you hear and read?
- ◆ Can you sort out the main ideas from the supportive details?
- ◆ Can you figure out the perspective of a particular writer/speaker?
- ◆ Can you express yourself clearly, concisely, correctly?
- ◆ Can you extract key points from what you read/hear?
- ◆ Can you handle complex information from a variety of sources?
- ◆ Can you conduct research (find information, synthesize/analyze/evaluate, use proper documentation techniques)?
- ◆ If given a visual (chart, graph, map, diagram) with a text, can you use *both* the visual *and* the text to interpret the information?

- Have you read from many different cultures?
- Can you adjust your reading rate, to suit the purpose?
- Can you adjust and manipulate your style of language, to suit the purpose and audience?
- Can you write reports, feature articles, etc.?
- Can you interpret and apply figurative language?
- Can you compare and contrast?
- Can you read between the lines?
- Can you make assumptions and test them, given new information?
- Have you read from many genres? Do you know how to recognize various genres, what to expect from them, how to distinguish among them?
- Can you discuss literature thematically (not just giving a plot summary) and can you use literary terminology in your discussion?
- Can you evaluate literature (or a speech) based upon certain criteria? Can you establish criteria for a given purpose of evaluation?
- Can you hear and appreciate the many voices of the English language?
- Can you discern and present a controlling idea in two or more similar (or seemingly dissimilar) works?
- Can you read the author/speaker's tone?
- Can you use and understand language presented in a variety or organizational patterns?
- Can you speak and write Standard English?
- Can you apply the conventions of Standard English effectively?

The Standards Portfolio

When we speak of the Standards portfolio, we are referring to a collection of work over the entire year, or even over more than 1 year, that attests to the student's progress toward the Standards. As the year progresses, the students keep their work, graded versions as well as some drafts, and they periodically review, revise, and reflect.

At given points during the year, students present the collection of organized representative samples of work. Viewed as a whole, the collection answers the questions: *What have I learned in English so far this year? What do I need to improve?*

The collection is not just greatest hits—it can display the worst as well as the best.

The collection should correspond to the Standards, so the students should be aware of the Standards, and be able to match their work to them. It can contain videotapes, audiotapes, photographs, sketches, charts, and graphs. It can have informal notes, reader response, even photocopies of passages out of novels that the student feels were particularly important in answering the questions: *What have I learned in English this year? Where do I need to improve?*

Because formative assessment depends on the partnership between teacher and student, students should be thoroughly familiar with the language of the Standards. They should be able to monitor their own progress on each of the Standards that the teacher addresses.

A Rubric for the Standards Portfolio

Content: *The portfolio consists of the required quantity and types of material.*

4____

3____

2____

1____

Organization: *The items are presented in a logical and orderly sequence, with the components clearly labeled.*

4____

3____

2____

1____

Presentation: *The portfolio is neat and attractive, representing care and pride in presentation.*

4____

3____

2____

1____

Reflection: *The reflective pieces show insight into your learning style, progress, and areas in need if improvement.*

4____

3____

2____

1___

Summary

The Standards work toward getting students to use the English language with fluency, variety, and flexibility. By *fluency*, we mean that students are able to express themselves in clear Standard English and to read English with sufficient speed, accuracy and expression to extract meaning from text. By *variety*, we mean that students are able to understand and produce the English language in more than one voice. And by *flexibility*, we mean that students are able to adjust their language to suit the purpose and audience.

Our formative assessments need to be grounded in the Standards, moving students along a continuum toward competency and excellence. The gradations of the continuum are spelled out on the rubric. In the next chapter, we will start designing formative assessments that will achieve this goal.

3

Rubrics

This chapter will tell you what you need to know about rubrics: how to design and use them not only as a way to score papers accurately and consistently, but also as a reliable guide for the students, so that they know what is expected from a task as they work through it:

- ◆ What is a rubric and how is it used by teachers and students?
- ◆ What are some common pitfalls of rubric use and design?
- ◆ What is the most efficient rubric design for English Language Arts formative assessments?
- ◆ What are various methods of setting up the rubric?
- ◆ How do we check a rubric for flaws?

What Is a Rubric and How Is It Used By Teachers and Students?

A rubric is a scoring guide: It tells the student and teacher what traits will be evaluated and presents a continuum of quality on those traits. A rubric is more than a guide for the teacher: It is a valuable learning tool for the student because it analyzes the task itself and the degrees of proficiency on the task. A rubric shows the student the traits that are being evaluated and what excellence in these traits looks like.

A rubric has three parts. First, it has *evaluative criteria*. These are the traits to be scored. Most English Language Arts rubrics consist of traits such as meaning (also called intent, ideas, content), development (also called substance, support, details, references, proof), organization, conventions (also called mechanics or presentation), word choice (also called diction, tone, or vocabulary), and sentence structure. Some rubrics combine word choice with sentence structure, under the heading of *language* or *style*. In addition, you might want to include something about the overall conditions of the paper: Is it neatly typed and proofread? Was it handed in on time? Does it have a proper heading? Margins? Spacing? Whatever is being evaluated must be stated forthrightly.

The second part of your rubric are the words to indicate quality on a continuum, such as *excellent, good, fair, unacceptable*. You should have either four or six levels on the quality continuum. If you have three or five, you'll find yourself huddling around that middle number, rather than making a definitive stand on the quality of a particular trait. For garden-variety performance tasks, I recommend a four-level rubric. For high stakes tasks, such as final exams or exhibitions, where you might have multiple scorers, you might want a rubric that is refined to accommodate six levels of a continuum from unacceptable to excellent.

The portion of the rubric for *word choice* might look like this:

Criteria/Levels	4. Excellent: *consistent*	3. Good: *emergent*	2. Fair: *inconsistent*	1. Unacceptable: *deficient*
Word Choice	◆ is varied, interesting, appropriate ◆ uses figurative language			

If you leave the boxes blank, as I've done, you have some room to write comments or give examples of weaknesses. Some teachers prefer to carry the wording throughout all of the boxes, thinking that doing so clarifies the specifications on each level.

The third part of your rubric is your *scoring strategy*. Here's where you decide how you are going to tally up your score for the total piece. You can consider each of the evaluative criteria (traits) equally, or you can work out a formula for weighting them. If you choose to use a *holistic strategy*, you will make an overall judgment and express it with a single number. If you choose a more time-consuming method, an *analytic strategy*, then you award a value to each trait, weighted or not, and calculate the result to arrive at a grade.

If the rubric is to have instructive value, the students need to have it as they work through the piece. They also need to take some responsibility to evaluate themselves and to refer to the traits as they work, just as anyone who builds something works with a set of specs. One good idea is to have the students submit the rubric along with the finished product, *with their own markings on the rubric*. They can even include a reflective piece prior to having you grade the work.

Rubrics are an indispensable tool for formative assessment because it is by looking at the rubric that the student and teacher can clearly see areas of need.

What Are Some Common Pitfalls in Rubric Use and Design?

You can find all manner of commercially prepared rubrics, as I present in this book, as well as rubrics "sent down" by State Education Departments. These may be useful to you, but if you are a novice, you'll need to get the feel of tailoring rubrics that you create yourself for formative assessment tasks. As you learn to create and judge the efficacy of rubrics, be wary of the following mistakes.

Mistake 1: Too Many Rubrics

When I first started using rubrics, I thought I should have a different rubric for each task that my students were doing. I began each one from scratch. If the result was a paperwork overload for me, imagine what it was for my students! Gradually, I learned that the traits that I was evaluating were more or less the same for almost everything. If you have too many rubrics, chances are that they are too task specific. The idea is *not* to spell out to the students exactly what they must do to get a high grade on a particular task. If our guidelines are overly specific, then we are giving the student too much information and not allowing her to think for herself. A good rubric is general enough to apply to more than one task.

Mistake 2: Generalities

On the other hand, if a rubric is too broad, it might do little more than state the obvious: a trait is good because it's good. Every trait on the rubric has to be teachable and manifest. In the "word choice" segment above, the words *varied, interesting, appropriate* are discrete and measurable. We aren't simply telling the students that their word choice has to be "well-chosen" or "sophisticated." The former is vague and circuitous; the latter is not only subjective, but misleading: not all "sophisticated" words are appropriate for the context. We aren't looking for a display of fancy words.

Mistake 3: Wordiness

If, in our quest for thoroughness and exactitude, we overwhelm the page with tiny lettering and full sentences, the rubric will simply not be used. It will be uninviting. Wordiness often happens when several teachers devise the rubric. It ends up having "something for everybody" and it looks it. I'm reminded of the maxim that "a camel is a horse designed by a committee." User-friendliness in the form of eye appeal and accessibility is paramount to a successful rubric. The Meaning heading for the new New York State Regents Exam in English looks like this for the three highest levels:

Quality	6 Responses at this level	5 Responses at this level	4 Responses at this level
Meaning: the extent to which the response exhibits sound understanding, interpretation, and analysis of the task and test(s)	♦ establish a controlling idea that reveals an in-depth analysis of both texts ♦ make insightful connections between the controlling idea, the ideas in each text, and the elements or techniques used to convey those ideas	♦ establish a controlling idea that reveals a thorough understanding of both texts ♦ make explicit connections between the ideas in each text and the elements or techniques used to convey those ideas	♦ establish a controlling idea that shows a basic understanding of the texts ♦ make few or superficial connections between the controlling idea, the ideas in the texts, and the elements or techniques used to convey those ideas

What you see here is the first three out of six boxes running horizontally on a rubric that has five qualities running vertically. When you squish all that language onto a single page, the result is formidable. Of course, this particular rubric is for a high stakes assessment, and teachers receive extensive training in its use, so it may not be as daunting as it seems. Still, we'd have to admit that, even if teachers were to develop proficiency on such a wordy rubric, only the most conscientious of *students* would be likely to make friends with it.

Here's how we present the same information more concisely:

Quality	6 Responses at this level show	5 Responses at this level show	4 Responses at this level show
Meaning: Does the writer understand, interpret, and analyze the task?	♦ in-depth analysis of task ♦ sharp insight into literary elements and techniques ♦ overt and subtle relationships between themes and details	♦ good understanding of task ♦ some insight into literary elements and techniques ♦ overt relationships between themes and details	♦ basic understanding of task ♦ basic understanding of literary elements or techniques ♦ basic understanding of relationships between themes and details

That's a word reduction of 33%, and we've also put the language into the vernacular, which brings us into the next mistake.

Mistake 5: Jargon

All professionals use esoteric language, but, just as one of our standards is to teach students how to suit their language to the audience, we have to suit ours to theirs. This means rejecting such phrases as "the extent to which the response exhibits direction, shape, and coherence" in favor of "the extent to which the writing follows an outline." It's easy to slip into edspeak, but we lose our audience when we do so. Fortunately, vernacular language takes up less space than jargon and makes for a roomier page.

There's a difference between rubrics created for large-scale, standardized assessments, such as state or national exams, and those created for classroom use. For the former, there will be more than one rater. The more finely calibrated the scale, the higher the likelihood of between-rater agreement (Popham, 1997). Such rubrics are for teacher, not student, use. We can always present a "translated" vernacular version of these rubrics, so that students can practice. For garden variety classroom rubrics, where only one teacher will be assessing the task, a four point rubric written in simple language is most likely to be used as a guide by students.

In "What's Right—What's Wrong—With Rubrics," James Popham (1997) sums up the choices: "…in almost all instances, lengthy rubrics probably can be reduced to succinct but far more useful versions for classroom instruction. Such abbreviated rubrics can still capture the key evaluative criteria needed to judge students' responses. Lengthy rubrics, in contrast, will gather dust."

What Is the Most Efficient Rubric Design for English Language Arts Performance Tasks?

Popham refers to rubrics as "instructional illuminators." So, a rubric should be simple to use, clear, and relevant not only to this particular task, but to the larger issues of thinking in the subject area. It is a consummation devoutly to be wished that the student come to internalize knowledge about quality traits so that they no longer need to consult the specs. For this to happen, we need to present rubrics that have consistent structure and language.

Let's consider a four-point rubric (*excellent, good, fair, unacceptable*) on five traits. We'll look at rubric designs for the two kinds of performance tasks described in Chapter 1: product (written and physical) and behavior (structured and spontaneous).

Rubric for a Written or Physical Product

The following are the writing traits to be considered in this rubric.

Addressing the Task

This writing trait evaluates the extent to which the student interpreted the question correctly. One of our biggest frustrations about the way our students write is that they don't give us what we asked for. Instead of addressing a thematic question, they summarize. Instead of tracing character development, they summarize. Instead of analyzing literary devices, they summarize. So, Job One is to stay focused. The task will use key verbs of higher-order thinking, such as *interpret, analyze, compare/contrast, develop, design, persuade, defend, critique, evaluate*. The key verb should then appear in the rubric. Key adjectives are *in-depth, insightful, perceptive*. If the task involves showing understanding of reading material, then the writer needs to express an understanding of the author's intent: the tone and purpose. If the student misinterpreted the question, lapsed into summary, or stayed at a superficial level of analysis, the lower level of the continuum would indicate these weaknesses.

Development

Development is also called substance, support, details, references, or proof. This part of the rubric evaluates the extent to which the writer provided sufficient relevant and specific information. Key nouns that you can use here are *reasons, examples, descriptions, statistics, quotations, references*. Key adjectives are *various, fully, thorough, relevant focused, multifaceted*. If the writer has strayed from the topic and included irrelevancies and redundancies, the lower levels of the continuum would be the place to indicate these weaknesses. Padding, the inclusion of deliberately wordy information used to give the illusion of substance, can be indicated here or under the *meaning* heading.

Organization

Organization is also called structure, order, or sequencing. This part of the rubric evaluates the extent to which the piece has structure, shape, logical flow, and transition. It takes into account the presence of paragraphing, topic sentences, transition, introduction, conclusion. Key nouns: *order, logic, progression, transition*. Key verbs: *lead, progress, link, connect, follow*. Structural flaws, such as the absence of topic sentences, and other such "qualities of chaos" as non sequiturs, lack of paragraphing, and absence of the expected parts of a writing piece would be noted in the lower ranges.

Word Choice

Word Choice is also called diction, style, tone, voice, fluency, vocabulary, or language. This part of the rubric evaluates the extent to which the piece shows control over diction and sentence structure, appropriateness of tone, varied and interesting vocabulary, and use of figurative language. Here is where we comment on whether sentence after sentence begins with the subject, creating a choppy effect. Here is also where skilled use of punctuation to achieve rhythm, ease of reading, conciseness, and control come in. We are also looking for language variety: ability to use synonyms where appropriate, ability to deploy a variety of punctuation marks, ability to manage many different kinds of grammatical structures. We're also looking for refinements and control of long sentences: parallel structure, subordination, contrasting elements. In terms of vocabulary, we're evaluating for appropriateness. Does the student understand when to use technical terms and when to use the vernacular? Does the student use elevated Latin- and Greek-based words as well as strong Anglo-Saxon words? Does it look as though this student is reaching out for new words? Do we see words that we've taught in class? Do we see literary terms? Is the figurative language fresh, or is it trite? Has the student tried using allusion? Is there a pithy title?

Word Choice is a comprehensive category. I'm tempted to break it in two: vocabulary and sentence structure. The only thing that keeps me from doing so is that I don't want my rubric to exceed one page, and I'm adhering to the advice of experts that a serviceable rubric should be limited to five criteria.

This is also where we consider the sense of audience. Has the student used slang in a formal essay? Has the student used a dry tone where the piece is meant to amuse? Does the student sound stuffy or stilted? Some students overdo this in their efforts to sound poetic, and they can sound cloying, like someone with too much perfume.

We should encourage students to use figurative language, humor, irony, allusion, and other gems of language which we point out in the literature that we teach.

Word choice also includes the qualities of conciseness and vigor. Here is where we indicate that we find awkward phrasing, passive voice, muddiness. We're noting sentences choked with word weeds, ramblers, overstatements, and empty statements.

Although there is a black line on the rubric to distinguish one evaluative criterion from its neighbor, the traits bleed into each other. Many of the atrocities described in the *Word Choice* category also apply to *Conventions*. When it comes to evaluating language it can be difficult to discriminate between a grammatical error and a stylistic error. What's grammatically perfect may be stylistically dead. Perhaps the best adjective to describe what we're looking for in word choice is *robust*. Robust language is strong, healthy, vivid, intense, and clear.

Conventions

Conventions are also called mechanics or presentation. This part of the rubric evaluates the extent to which the student uses the correct protocols of standard written English. That includes spelling, punctuation, capitalization, subject–verb agreement, correct verb forms, pronoun–antecedent agreement, correct pronoun case and number, and other such matters. It also includes presentation: that the piece is handed in on time, on the proper type of paper, stapled or clipped as specified, bearing the proper heading, with regulation fonts, spacing, and margins. It also includes proper documentation techniques on a research paper.

Physical Product

The above descriptions apply to writing tasks, but they can be easily adapted to other performance tasks. For a physical product, such as a decorated box of props or a book cover design, you could replace *development* with *design* and include such visual aspects as color choice, dominant image, secondary images, symbolism. Most physical products do have some verbal component, even if it's just a brief explanation, orally or on an index card. A physical product in an English class has much in common with a work of advertising, where the language is succinct and pithy. Often, the project is humorous in tone.

A physical product can easily miss the mark where *meaning* is concerned. Its literary value can be lost to the intricacy of the artwork. If students are making a model of the Globe Theater, there should be a verbal component wherein they bring in the impact of design on performance. They could talk about the implications of having no curtain, or no amplification. They could note that, in Shakespearean plays, the actor would often turn himself around during monologues, playing to all sides of the house. Or, they could point out several examples of the bawdy lines that were pitched to the groundlings, as opposed to the lofty speeches written to please the monarch. The task has to be carefully designed so that English Language Arts standards are met, which is why we *begin* performance task design with the standards. Whether it be a classroom poster or a soundtrack, meaning, in terms of the standards, is still foremost: Did the student meet the specs? Were the specs in line with English Language Arts standards?

You may combine the categories of organization and development for a physical product. Everything assembled to convey meaning has to have some schematic structure. Is there logical subordination of details to main idea? Does the piece consist of multiple elements, such as a decorated props box? Are the items numbered, clustered, labeled, presented in some order?

Lastly, for *Conventions*, presentation can be called *Workmanship* or *Detailing*. The product can't be displayed if it has gross errors, is messy, or unsturdy.

A Word on Interdisciplinary Projects

The headings of *Meaning, Development, Organization, Language*, and *Conventions* cover the territory that you need to assess, as well as to instruct, in written and physical products in English class. So much the better if you can achieve consistency of language within the English department. It's worth trying to interest your colleagues in the other disciplines to use this terminology as well. In writing a lab report, for example, these headings apply, as they do for any social studies report. As we've seen, we have many synonyms, and, although students should develop flexibility, they shouldn't have the sense that it's an altogether different ball game from one class to the next. Science teachers don't necessarily care about literary techniques in their lab reports, but they do have a word choice component: they are looking for proper terminology and concise wording. If the wording is not focused, then the message isn't clear, and if the message isn't clear, then the science teacher doesn't know if the student understands the meaning.

Rubrics for Structured or Spontaneous Behavior

Panel discussions, prepared speeches, dramatic readings, rehearsed scripted scenes, and planned interviews are examples of performance tasks for which we assess structured behavior.

When assessing behavior, we can combine *meaning and development* as the first criterion: Did the students stay focused on the task? Unskilled or unprepared students will drift away from the topic or lapse into repetition. If the performance is based on scripted material, the meaning and development would be manifest in how the lines are delivered to convey meaning.

Whether organization is an appropriate heading for a behavioral task depends on the extent to which the student had to do the organizing. Organization is not a factor in a dramatic reading or scripted scene, but it is definitely a factor in a planned interview.

In assessing a behavioral task, I prefer the term *language use* to *word choice*. Language use refers not only to vocabulary level, but also to habits of speech: Is the style free of word weeds such as *like, ya know, um*? Is the delivery audible and distinct? If the student is explaining something in her own words, is she using proper terminology or relying on lazy fillers, such as "the thingy" and "the whatsis." The rules for spoken English are more relaxed than those for standard written English, but a reasonable level of colloquial English usage would be expected.

The *conventions* of a behavioral task are the conventions of speaking etiquette: eye contact, a businesslike posture, a facial expression that shows interest and undivided attention to other speakers, speaking in turn, showing enthusiasm.

For assessment of spontaneous behavior, you need a different kind of rubric. By spontaneous behavior, we mean habits of classroom citizenship, which can also be called class participation or attitude. We shouldn't overlook this aspect of performance even though it may seem elusive. Years ago, all that counted were percentages on a test. But that way of thinking reduces education to a "factory model." Today, we know that assessment can be more sophisticated and can be based on a variety of factors. A test or a task will never cover all the territory of what a student knows and can do. That is why we should include spontaneous behavior that does, or does not, manifest learning.

How do you know that a student takes learning seriously and is an active member of your class? Attitude and effort usually play a part, especially in the lower grades, in overall assessment. Behaviors such as handing work in on time, asking appropriate questions, offering responses, offering to read aloud, staying on task, setting a good example, having good attendance, being willing to lead, and seeking assistance are all observable signs that a student is reaching out to learn in your class.

In addition to these public behaviors are personal behaviors (habits of mind) such as keeping an organized notebook, writing due dates in a daily planner, coming to class on time and prepared with materials, making up work missed during absences. All of these behaviors fall under the heading of *conscientious work habits*. When we consider how important such behaviors are in the workplace, we see the value of including them in classroom assessment. Qualities such as persistence, willingness to listen to others, willingness to take intellectual risks, meticulousness, and attention to detail are all behaviors that we can and should assess from time to time.

Finally, we can observe and assess certain metacognitive habits. Does the student show an interest in learning from your comments and corrections? Is he sincere about improving his skills, or does he care only about the grade? When he writes a reflective piece, does he show insight into his learning style? Does he have an awareness of his strengths and weaknesses? Does he followup on suggestions for improvement?

A sturdy structure for an English Language Arts rubric evaluates for meaning, development, organization, word choice, and conventions. For ordinary classroom assessments, a four-level rubric (excellent, good, fair, unacceptable) will suffice. We will probably refine the rubric to six levels if there is to be more than one reader on a high-stakes test. We can adapt the basic criteria to other types of performance tasks, such as physical projects or dramatic presentations. Additionally, we can have a rubric that assesses for spontaneous behavior, the habits of mind that students exhibit and that are a part of their learning. Rubrics are most effective when they are user friendly, predictable, and concise.

What Are Various Methods of Setting Up the Rubric?

You can set up your rubric with *boxes going across* the page, or you can work with a *checklist going down* the page. You can also combine these two formats. We present various formats because some teachers prefer one over another.

Format One: Boxes

Scoring Guide: Written Task

Criteria/Levels	Excellent: consistent	Good: emergent	Fair: inconsistent	Unacceptable: deficient
Addressing the Task	♦ sharp focus on the question ♦ insight, depth	←——————————→		♦ missing the point of the question ♦ stating the obvious
Development	♦ reasons, examples, explanations ♦ strong paragraph structure	←——————————→		♦ lacking support ♦ redundant ♦ irrelevant ♦ too brief or too long

Criteria/Levels	Excellent: consistent	Good: emergent	Fair: inconsistent	Unacceptable: deficient
Organization	♦ all components present ♦ strong transitions ♦ coherence	←	→	♦ lacking transition
Word Choice	♦ varied, interesting, appropriate vocabulary/ sentence structure ♦ figurative language ♦ clarity ♦ conciseness	←	→	♦ flat language ♦ wordiness ♦ incoherent sentences
Conventions	♦ free of errors ♦ careful proofreading ♦ careful presentation	←	→	♦ many errors in basic usage ♦ not proofread ♦ careless presentation

With a few minor adjustments on the wording, the same rubric could be set up vertically.

Format Two: Vertical

Addressing the Task: The writer maintains a sharp focus; content shows insight and depth.

4_____

3_____

2_____

1_____

Development: The writer gives sufficient reasons, examples, descriptions, or explanations to fully support key points.

4_____

3_____

2_____

1_____

Organization: The writer includes all component parts: introduction, well-developed paragraphs with transitions, conclusion. The piece is coherent, with all sentences relevant and presented in a logical sequence.

4_____

3_____

2_____

1_____

Word Choice: The writer uses vocabulary and sentence structure which are varied, interesting, and appropriate. The writer uses figurative language effectively. Sentences are clear and concise.

4_____

3_____

2_____

1_____

Conventions: The writer shows full control of spelling, capitalization, punctuation, and usage. The presentation is neat and conforms to specifications.

4_____

3_____

2_____

1_____

The advantage of the above style is that you have more room to write comments that justify your checkmarks or refer the student to specific segments of the piece. Also, you may prefer the full sentence, stipulating what you require at the level of excellence, as opposed to the brevity of words that is necessary in the box rubric. The box rubric seems to be favored for standardized tests where raters will not be making comments that the students will see.

The following rubric combines these two forms.

Format Three: Combined Form

Scoring Guide	4	3	2	1
Addressing the Task: Interpreting the question correctly				
Doing exactly what the task asks for _____				
Staying focused_____				
Showing depth and insight_____				

Scoring Guide	4	3	2	1
Development: Providing sufficient support				
Explanations and detail_____				
Examples and reasons_____				
Facts and figures_____				

Scoring Guide	4	3	2	1
Organization: Having a logical sequence				
Introduction:_____				
Well-developed paragraphs with topic sentences____				
Transition_____				
Conclusion_____				
Coherence (all pieces are related) _____				

Scoring Guide	4	3	2	1
Word Choice: Interesting vocabulary and sentence structure				
Variety:_____				
Appropriateness:_____				
Figurative Language_____				
Clarity and conciseness_____				

Scoring Guide	4	3	2	1
Conventions: Correctness and presentation				
Spelling:_____				
Capitalization: _____				
Punctuation:_____				
Grammar usage:_____				
Attractive and careful presentation _____				

It takes a little while to get used to rubric-based grading. You will tailor the style and content of your rubrics to fit your thinking and teaching style. Using a rubric eliminates the quandary of not "knowing what to say" on a student's paper. Although you can certainly write additional comments, using a rubric saves you time in the long run.

These rubrics assume equal value for all criteria. You can manipulate the value of a given criterion for a given task—sometimes, you place great value on language use; other times, on organization.

Checking Your Rubric for Flaws

You won't really know if your rubric is flawed until you start to use it, and then the flaws will jump out at you and you'll wonder how you could have missed them. As with proofreading, another pair of eyes is likely to spot glaring errors that you are blind to. That is why the following questions are best addressed among colleagues, rather than by yourself:

- Is every skill teachable and demonstrable? Can you follow up with students who show deficiency in each skill?
- Does the rubric reflect instruction?
- Is there too much jargon? Does it speak in a language style that students will understand?
- Does it cover the overarching thinking skills of the task, rather than its *specifics*?
- Will the student be a better thinker as a result of it?
- Is it as concise as it can possibly be?
- Is it not more than one page, with typeface large enough to read easily?

Summary

A rubric is successful if it sharpens the task and its expectations without being overly explicit. Because you and your students need to work hand in glove with the rubric, it needs to be a part of instruction from start to finish, not an afterthought. The rubric should tell the student what the difference is between work that is acceptable and that which is excellent.

As we design rubrics, we focus on content and skills, and that brings us into state and national learning Standards: what do we want our students to know and be able to do? Those concepts and competencies are enumerated by State Education Departments as well as by the NCTE/IRA (National Council of Teachers of English/International Reading Association).

Part II

Applications

4

Formative Assessments for Reading Comprehension

When you select reading material for a class, how do you know if students can comprehend it? How do you know what supports to provide for students who can't extract meaning from text without outside assistance or strategies? When you complete a lengthy reading experience, how do you know if your students' reading skills have improved?

In this chapter, I'll show you ten specific formative assessments that will give you and your students information about how well they can comprehend *the text in front of them.* I stress this because I know that you can obtain statistical information about your students' performance on standardized tests of reading comprehension. And you can apply a readability formula. Most of these are based on sentence length and number of words having more than two syllables.

So why can't you just refer to the standardized test scores and readability formulas as your indicators of reading comprehension? First, your standardized test scores don't factor in two of the most important requisites for reading comprehension: prior knowledge and interest in the subject. When a student reads some passages and answers questions on a standardized test, the student's comprehension level may differ from when she is reading the latest Harry Potter novel, a story about which she has a lot of prior knowledge and interest. Second, the common readability formulas don't take anything into account except sentence and word length. The information in the text could be very abstract, the dialogue and narration can be written in a dialect that the student is not familiar with, or the multisyllabic words could be commonly known ones. So, while the standardized test scores and readability formulas do yield *some* information, there are certainly better ways to assess whether or not the students sitting in your class right now can extract meaning from the text that they are holding in their hands right now.

Once you've done a formative assessment for text in current use, you'll know who needs intervention. Interventions to enhance reading comprehension will be discussed after the formative assessments are presented below:

Reading Comprehension: Process and Product

The *process of reading* refers to the reader's ability to decode and understand the text as eyes move across the page. The *product of reading* is the ability to remember and apply what has been read; that is, the evidence that the reader has extracted the author's intended meaning from the text, expanding the reader's knowledge. Another way of putting this is that the process of reading is the *ability to be smart* while reading, and the product of reading is the extent to which we've *stayed smart* as a result of reading.

Formative Assessments for Basic Comprehension

What follows are several assessments to determine how well students can comprehend the text in current use.

Five Easy Questions (Speed and Accuracy)

Fluency in reading is determined by three factors: accuracy, speed, and reading with expression. I learned about this simple but powerful assessment, which I'm calling "Five Easy Questions," from *A Handbook for Differentiated Instruction for Middle and High Schools* (Larchmont, NY: Eye On Education, 2005). Here's how it works:

- *Step One (preparation by teacher):* The teacher selects a random page or two from the text in current use and reads it, timing herself carefully. (Read at a slow pace, to simulate the rate of a student, who would be reading this for the first time.)

- *Step Two (preparation by teacher):* The teacher composes 5 basic comprehension questions that span the page.

- *Step Three (class activity):* The teacher asks the students to read the page or pages and time themselves. After reading the page(s), the students answer the five basic comprehension questions with or without looking back at the page(s). The students also list the words from the passage that are unfamiliar to them.

- *Step Four (assessment):* The teacher analyzes the results, plotting student's names on the chart, according to the graphic below:

Reading Comprehension Assessment

Which of my students need additional support to read the text independently?

Names of students who:	Names of students who:	Names of students who:
1. Read significantly slower than the average rate of speed 2. Have more than two errors in basic comprehension 3. Identify five or more unknown words in the text sample	1. Read at the average rate of speed 2. Have not more than two errors in basic comprehension 3. Identify fewer than five unknown words in the text sample	1. Read significantly faster than the average rate of speed 2. Have no errors in basic comprehension 3. Identify only one or two unknown words in the text sample

Supports:

◆ Provide more visuals

◆ Establish expectations before reading

◆ Provide guiding questions

◆ Establish a purpose for reading

◆ Pronounce unfamiliar words

This formative assessment is easily manageable and yields important, comparative information about the amount of support that students will need for both comprehension and vocabulary. It provides us with a visual that will help us group students according to their needs and differentiate instruction.

Reading Aloud (Expression)

We know that reading with expression is part of fluency. If you have reason to believe that a student reads fluently based on another formative assessment, or based on your observations or data, then you don't need to assess for expressive reading, especially as doing so will be time intensive. Listen to students read aloud passages in the current text. Deficient readers will not want to do this publicly, so find a way to work privately with them. Try reading together with the student, alternating sentences. Some teachers arrange reading dyads (partnerships) and listen around the room as students read aloud to each other.

Reading expressively has several components:

♦ *Pauses:* Does the reader take cues from punctuation, pausing appropriately for commas, end marks, ends of paragraphs? Equally important, does the reader *not* pause just because it's the end of a line? The ability to pause according to punctuation is particularly important in reading poetry and Shakespeare. Most novices to Shakespeare drop their voices and pause at the end of lines, rather than being guided by punctuation.

♦ *Pitch:* Does the reader raise his or her voice appropriately to signify questions? Does he or she read with appropriate rises and falls in pitch, rather than in a monotone?

♦ *Rhythm:* Effective readers render a sense of rhythm in prose as well as poetry and oratory. Rhythm can be created through repetitions of words and phrases.

♦ *Volume:* Does the reader read with enough volume to be heard clearly? Poor readers often mask their inaccuracies under an inaudible mumble.

♦ *Emphasis:* Reading with proper emphasis refers not only to emphasizing the accented syllables in individual words, but also to emphasizing words, usually verbs, that should be emphasized in sentences. When sentences begin with coordinating conjunctions, those coordinating conjunctions (and, but, so, yet, etc.) often invite emphasis.

♦ *Characterization:* When reading dialogue, does the reader capture the intended voice and language style of the speakers?

♦ *Overcoming stumbling blocks, such as unfamiliar words:* It's important to note what the reader does when coming across words that are unknown or hard to pronounce. Does the reader seem to use word components and patterns as a clue to pronunciation?

If you already know that you are working with a student who has deficits in reading, you might want the student to read the text again to see if expressiveness improves after the student already has baseline knowledge.

Cloze

The cloze procedure is for assessing reading comprehension as well as for improving it. In the cloze procedure, students are asked to supply words that have been deliberately deleted from the text. Usually, every fifth to tenth word is deleted. You can delete random words (such as every fifth word), or you may delete words selectively, leaving in the prepositions, conjunctions, and other structural supports within the sentence. You can supply a word bank or multiple choice selection. The cloze procedure is often used in standardized reading comprehension tests.

From the cloze procedure, you can find out if students would select a word that gives meaning to text not only semantically (Does the word selected indicate that the student understands what that word means?) but also grammatically (Does the word selected indicate that the student has a sense of how English words are used in sentence?) and stylistically (Does the word selected indicate that the student perceives cues about formal or informal language register?).

A variant of the cloze procedure, which some prefer, is called the C-test. Rather than deleting every fifth or tenth word, as the cloze procedure does, in the C-test, you actually delete the latter half of every second word. So that the reader gets the context of the piece as a whole, you leave the first and last sentence of the passage intact. Here's what the C-test might look like:

> "One cool autumn evening, Bob L., a young professional, returned home from a trip to the supermarket to find his computer gone. Gone! All so- of cr- thoughts ra- through h- mind: H- it be- stolen? H- it be- kidnapped? H- searched h- house f- a cl- until h- noticed a sm- piece o- printout pa- stuck un- a mag- on h- refrigerator do-. His he- sank a- he re- this sim- message: can't continue, file closed, bye." *(From http://exchanges.state.gov/forum/vols/vol31/no1/p35.htm)*

For the C-test, you do not supply a word bank or multiple choices. The student fills in the words, cued by his or her knowledge of the English language. The C-test is often used to determine placement in programs for nonnative speakers.

Recognizing Accurate Paraphrase

If you've comprehended a passage, you can explain it in your own words. A corollary is that if you've comprehended a passage, you should be able to distinguish an accurate paraphrase from an inaccurate one. After reading a passage, the reader is given four possible paraphrases and asked to identify the best one. One of the paraphrases would be accurate but incomplete; one would be accurate, but would contain more information than could be learned from the passage; one would contain inaccurate information; and one would be the correct choice.

Summarizing

A simple test for comprehension is the ability to write a summary. We can prompt the summary by using the chart below. Students can express their knowledge either in a traditional paragraph, or in a labeled diagram of the action. Either way, they should incorporate all of the information from the chart.

Summary Chart

Name: _____   Date: _____

Class: _____

Take notes in the columns of the chart on the key information in the chapter.
Use accurate character names and place names.

Transform your notes into a one-paragraph summary of the chapter.

Chapter	Who?	What?	When?	Where?	How?

Word Discrimination

One of the identifying features of deficient readers is that they tend to ignore the middle of words and can easily fail to see the difference between words that begin and end with the same syllable. Given the words in the columns below, the deficient reader could easily think they are all the same in each group.

Word Discrimination

Deficient readers are likely to miss the difference in these look-alike words

entourage encourage	feckless freckles	extrusion extraction	description discretion
apparent abhorrent	tropical topical	intimidate intimate	commended commanded
convenience contrivance	compensation compassion	patriarchy peculiarly particularly	mandatory mendacity
destitute desuetude	decision declension definition		component compartment

Ascertain Prior Knowledge

Ascertain prior knowledge with either a KWL chart or a set of questions that you think might determine prior knowledge. Prior knowledge is widely regarded as the key determiner of reading comprehension: "…what students *already know* about the content is one of the strongest indicators of how well they will learn new information relative to the content" (Marzano, 2006, p. 1, emphasis in original). We can ascertain background knowledge formally, by giving students questions to answer, or informally, by listening to their responses as they discuss the topic in cooperative learning groups. We can also use motivating activities such as games, storytelling, and skits to ascertain prior knowledge. In any case, we do need to fill in gaps in necessary background knowledge either by direct, whole-class teaching, or by providing resources and experiences that will prepare students to receive new information.

Quality of Questions

The kinds of questions that students have after reading will give you insight to the depth of their understanding. Student-made tests are an excellent formative assessment. Have the students compose all or part of a test on what they've read, with the understanding that you will accept some of their questions on a real test if the questions are good enough to make the cut. (You'll see that some students have a poor sense of what kinds of questions a teacher might ask on a test.) After they've composed their questions, they should categorize them by their content and level of complexity. The point of doing the question corners is *not* to answer the questions, just to pose them. You will see by the location of the questions on the page the extent to which a student is able to engage in higher level thinking. (The questions on the right side of the following figure represent higher level thinking than those on the left.)

Question Corners

Name: _____   Date: _____

Class: _____

What kinds of questions am I asking?
(For Student-Made Questions)

(Literal questions)   (Interpretative questions)

    What?   Why?
    Where?   How?
    When?

(Analytical questions)   (Speculative questions)

    Which one?   What next?
    What kind?   So what?
    What part of?   What if?

Word Component Charts

You need to know the extent to which your students can analyze unfamiliar words based on components: prefixes, roots, suffixes, and combining forms. The ability to put together this "word kit" is crucial to comprehending academic language. The unfamiliar words in academic language rely heavily on Latin and Greek word components. Given an incomplete chart, students are asked to use their knowledge of word components to make educated guesses to fill in the blanks.

Give 3 points for words that students can define; 2 points for words that exist in the English language even if the student can't define them; 1 point for words that don't exist but nevertheless make sensible use of word components.

Word Components Chart I

Name: _____ Date: _____

Class: _____

Write the words that you've heard of that would logically fill in the chart.
(Note: Not all the blanks should be filled in.)

	-tract	-struct	-port	-verse	-pel
pre-					
re-			report		
un-					
a, ab-				averse	
sub-	subtract				
de-					
pro-					propel
ob-					
con-		construct			

Word Components Chart II

Name: _____ Date: _____

Class: _____

Write the words that you've heard of that would logically fill in the chart.
(Note: Not all of the blanks should be filled in.)

	-tion	-ment	-able -ible	-er, or	-ence -ance
tract-	attraction			contractor	
port-					
vert-					
pel-					
struct-					
script-					
cred-					
spec-					
duct-					

Mini-Mysteries

The "mini-mystery" is subgenre that combines the detective story with the brain teaser and a reading comprehension passage. The mini-mystery is a high-interest, engaging way to assess and improve reading comprehension because it forces the reader to pay attention to details. Using accessible language and familiar subjects, the mini-mystery is a short (usually not more than about 750 words) narrative with a simple plot. The reader is given a story in which something is amiss: A witness falsely reports events, and the reader has find inconsistencies or impossibilities to determine where the story fails the credibility test. To do this, the reader has to read astutely, as the clues are usually masked within casual conversation between the witness and the investigator. The reader has to say: "Hey, wait a minute! That can't have happened that way!" The mini-mystery usually has the following elements:

1. A crime

2. An investigator

3. One or more witnesses recounting their version of events

4. Clues, such as scientific facts or sequence of events

5. An inconsistency that the reader must infer

6. A resolution, in which the investigator solves the crime, but the reader is left to figure out how the investigator put the clues together to do so

Mini-mysteries can be used to assess for reading comprehension of details, inference, and background knowledge. For you to use the mini-mystery as formative assessment, you must have insight as to why the reader was unable to solve the mystery, which is why students need to explain their reasoning. Their explanations will tell you whether they are reading all of the information, making inferences, drawing conclusions, understanding key vocabulary, using context clues, synthesizing new information with background knowledge.

Having students read and solve the occasional mini-mystery will not do much to improve reading comprehension or instill the habit of careful, active reading. Nor will sporadic experiences with mini-mysteries give you useful information about reading needs of individual students. But if students were to read and solve mini-mysteries consistently and systematically, graduating from one level of difficulty to the next, their reading comprehension and critical thinking skills can improve significantly. I recommend giving students three levels of mini-mysteries, in sets of ten mini-mysteries on each level. You may pre-assess by having students complete one or two mini-mysteries on each of the three levels. Put students to work on the level that will represent a manageable challenge based on the pre-assessment. Speed should be a factor. Time students on the pre-assessment, using the average reading rate of your class as the pacesetter. Have students read and solve one mini-mystery per day while you continue to build reading skills with the other literary activities and readings that you normally do.

The following is a guide for students to chart their progress as they work their way through a series of mini-mysteries.

My Mini-Mystery Track Record

Name: _____   Date: _____

Class: _____

Level: _____

Title of Mini-Mystery	Date	How much time did you spend to read and solve it?	Were you able to solve it correctly?

If a student's progress is significantly slower than the pace of the class, and they are already working at the easiest level, here are some interventions that might help:

- *Encourage metacognition:* Ask the student which, if any, of the following reading strategies he or she is employing to read and solve the mini-mysteries:

  - Rereading

  - Skimming for main idea before reading every word

  - Reading in a quiet, well-lit environment with no distractions and when feeling alert

  - Visualizing

- *Find out if it's a vocabulary problem:* Do an assessment of the vocabulary to see if there are a critical number of words that the student may not know. Ask the student to tell you about these words. Have the student scan for new words and then look them up in a simplified dictionary before reading.

- *Is it a background knowledge problem?* A lot of mini-mystery solutions depend on the reader's recognition of anachronisms. For example, a photograph or painting predates an item that appears in the picture. Many depend on a rudimentary knowledge of physics or geography. If a lack of background knowledge is the problem, try to find a wider variety of mini-mysteries.

Ask your library-media specialist to help you collect a library of mini-mysteries at different levels of difficulty and on a wide variety of subjects. Avoid the ones that are based on mathematical knowledge or science that cloud the issue of pure reading comprehension.

Don't confuse the kind of mini-mysteries that can assess reading with brain teasers that sometimes go under the name of "Minute Mysteries" or "puzzles for lateral thinking." It isn't that such puzzles aren't worthwhile; it's just that they call for thinking that goes beyond what we're assessing for. Here are a few sources that are appropriate for using mini-mysteries as formative assessment of reading comprehension.

- http://kids.mysterynet.com/comprehension.

- http://www.justriddlesandmore.com/mysterycorner.html

- http://www.isd77.k12.mn.us/schools/dakota/mystery/contents. html (A collection of mini-mysteries written by eighth grade students at Dakota Meadows Middle School in North Mankato, MN.)

Summary

The chart below shows you at a glance how to use the ten formative assessments discussed in this chapter.

10 Formative Assessments for Reading Comprehension

Assessment	What can you find out?		How can you respond?
Five Easy questions	Basic comprehension at a literal level	Words that students identify as unknown	
Reading aloud	Speed and accuracy for fluency	Ability to break down long words	Model reading aloud; Choral reading
Cloze	Basic comprehension	Whether a word makes sense grammatically in a sentence	Provide a word bank
Recognizing accurate paraphrase	Ability to recognize main ideas	Ability to recognize synonyms	Have students write paraphrase; paraphrase as a class activity
Summarizing	Ability to express main ideas	Ability to change wording	Provide a partial summary or a word bank
Word discrimination	Ability to attend to the middle part of long words	Understanding the importance of Latin word roots	Teach word roots; build words out from roots to affixes
Ascertain prior knowledge	Whether students have enough information to comprehend	Whether students know key vocabulary	Provide resources or give direct instruction
Quality of questions	Ability to read analytically	Ability to extend content beyond the literal level	Provide question stems for higher level questions
Word Component Charts	Knowledge of prefixes, suffixes, roots	Understanding of patterns as they apply to words in English	Teach prefixes, suffixes, and roots explicitly
Mini-Mysteries	Ability to make inferences	Discipline to read every word	Practice visualization while reading

5

Formative Assessment for Writing

The goal of writing is to communicate a worthwhile idea clearly to meet the needs of the writer's intended audience. The ability to express oneself in writing is essential for success in all subject areas and throughout life. Writing is how students "connect the dots" in their understandings, how they make their own thinking visible to themselves and others. Mastery of writing is a lifelong pursuit. Summative assessments in writing evaluate the written product against a set of criteria for a given level that students on a grade level are expected to achieve. Formative assessments in writing are supposed to give students encouragement about their successes as well as a small number of accessible goals for the next attempt. Key words in the previous sentence are *small number* and *accessible* goals.

As an English teacher it is not your job to correct every single error or lapse that you see in every piece of writing. If you were learning any complex skill, you wouldn't expect your coach to point out every imperfection. You would appreciate encouragement and acknowledgement for your improvements and a few pointers that will help you to keep up the good work. So it is with you and your students: Think in terms of their ability, as individuals, to move to the *next* step, not to make unrealistic leaps all at once.

Three Kinds of Writing: Three Kinds of Formative Assessment

I like to divide the subject of writing into three categories: workshop writing, writing for assessment, and writing to learn.

Workshop Writing

I define true workshop writing as writing in which the students pursue their own topic, a topic of interest to them. They are writing because they have something to say to someone. This kind of writing has an authentic feel—the writer wishes to communicate. The desire to communicate drives the piece. In workshop writing, the piece emerges like a piece of sculpture from a block of clay. The writer has some idea at the outset of what the piece is going to be, but it may seem to "write itself" as the writer nurses it along.

Another characteristic of workshop writing is that it takes place within a community of writers (the class) who share ideas and give each other constructive feedback. The feedback may take the form of conversations between writers as they read each other's drafts. Many teachers choose to provide guiding questions for readers.

True workshop writing thrives within an atmosphere of mutual support between the teacher and the writers and among the writers for each other. This mutual support for the developing work culminates in a celebratory classroom ritual as the final pieces are published. Publication can be in the form of read-alouds, postings for the classroom or hallway, formal compilations, and/or portfolios.

Formative assessment can take place to guide the students at multiple points in the writing process.

Pre-Writing I (Brainstorming)

This is the stage in which the writer expresses possible ideas in profusion (brainstorming). Brainstorming is supposed to be uncensored because it thrives on the notion that *any* idea can lead to a great things. Brainstorming should be noisy and messy but can nevertheless bring forth something that is assessable. The fruits of the brainstorming session may look like one or more of the following:

- Lists of words, phrases, pictures
- Webs, bubbles
- Trial sentences

Brainstorming is characterized by informality and loose, if any, organizational structures. (Don't confuse brainstorming with more structured formats such as graphic organizers or outlines. These are forms that brainstorming will take later in the process, as writers turn their brainstorm "possibilities" into graphically organized "probabilities.") Sometimes, students loosen up when given alternative media for brainstorming. Instead of traditional paper, try laying newspaper across their desks and giving them markers or even finger paint (yes, finger paint!). Invite students to the board and have them use the big spaces to brainstorm. Let them work in pairs or groups.

Assess brainstorming in accordance with its spirit; that is, assess it broadly, with a single question: *Is there evidence of a wide range of ideas, words, phrases, and nonverbal representations on the topic?*

In addition to what you read on paper (or the board), observe the students as they brainstorm. Good brainstorming has a sense of urgency, energy, and, most of all, fluency. The student who agonizes over every word isn't in the right frame of mind for brainstorming. That student needs your help to lighten up and let it flow. Remind the student that there's no right or wrong in a brainstorm session.

Pre-Writing II (Statement of Main Idea)

Although a workshopped piece may well take its own direction, as mentioned earlier, the writer does need to begin with a general notion of intent, just as an artist has a mental image of what she wishes to paint as she sketches out her vision. Have the students express their main idea in a single sentence. Assess the sentence for completeness and meaningfulness.

In Pamela Dykstra's *An Easy Guide to Writing* (2006), the bicycle is a metaphor for a complete sentence: The "subject wheel" tells "Who or what?" and the "predicate wheel" tells "What about it?" Once students establish a simple subject and predicate for their statement of main idea, they can elaborate by getting more specific or even compounding either "wheel." You can even give students an actual illustration or cutout of a bicycle and have them write their subject and predicate on the front and back wheels.

Pre-Writing III (Planning)

This is the stage where the writer decides what kind of graphic organizer(s) to use to trim and fit their ideas into a recognizable pattern. Typically, the patterns will be those of the major rhetorical modes:

- Narrative
- Sensory description
- Classification, with definitions and examples
- Cause and effect
- Comparison–contrast
- Steps in a process

The figures that follow can be used as graphic organizers to help students understand the major text patterns.

Narrative

Name: _____ Date: _____

Class: _____

Setting: (Where and When)

Key phrases to describe the setting:

Main character:

Supporting characters:

The main character wants_____,

but_____

because, so_____

Sensory Description

Name: _____ Date: _____

Class: _____

What are the phrases that describe the sights?

What are the phrases the describe the sounds?

What are the phrases that describe the textures?

What are the phrases that describe the feel and smell of the air?

If you were a filmmaker, what would we see in your panoramic shots?

What would we see in your tight close-ups of details?

Cause and Effect

Name: _____   Date: _____

Class: _____

One way to write a sentence that expresses cause and its effect is to begin the sentence with *because*. When you begin a sentence with *because*, the sentence must have two parts, with a comma after the first part:

Because of A, B happens.

Write a sentence that explains a cause and its effect.

Because_____,

_____.

Definition

Name: _____   Date: _____

Class: _____

_____   is

(subject, expressed as a noun)

_____   THAT

(Place the subject into a general category.)

_____

_____

Name the specific characteristics of the subject that distinguish it from other members of its category.

Example

Name: _____   Date: _____

Class: _____

is an example of

_____

_____

(its features) { _____

_____

_____

Comparison/Contrast

between _____ and _____

Name: _____ Date: _____

Class: _____

	How they are similar	How they are different
Feature:		
Feature:		
Feature:		
Feature:		

Classification

Name: _____ Date: _____

Class: _____

Steps in a Process

Name: _____   Date: _____

Class: _____

Steps:

In the pre-writing stage, students should choose whichever of the graphic organizers, or some combination, best suits the expression of their ideas. Using a graphic organizer is like pushing clay into a mold: what emerges has a recognizable form with boundaries.

A glance at the graphic organizer will give you formative assessment as to whether your young writers are facing in the right direction, saddled with enough equipment to get moving.

Pre-Writing IV (Word/Phrase Inventory)

Every topic has what linguists call a "notional set" of words. A topic's notional set is the set of words and phrases that are likely to be used together to communicate about that topic. The pre-writing phase is the perfect opportunity to proliferate vocabulary by leading students in the creation of a list of words and phrases that will serve as an inventory for the writing piece that they are about to begin. In workshop writing, the word inventory will by individualized, as the topics are self-selected.

If the writer generates the word inventory as a list, she might miss opportunities to categorize and find subordinating relationships. Therefore, I prefer word cluster diagrams, word flows, and semantic maps.

Use the figures that follow to cue students as they generate the words that will be useful in an upcoming writing task.

Cluster Word Inventory

Name: _____ Date: _____

Class: _____

Topic: _____

Word Cluster 1
Subcategory:

Word Cluster 2
Subcategory:

Word Cluster 3
Subcategory:

Directions: Decide on three different subcategories and write word clusters
that might be used to talk about each one.

Word Flow

Name: _____ Date: _____

Class: _____

Directions: Write as many words and phrases that you can think of for your topic.

Semantic Mapping

Name: _____ Date: _____

Class: _____

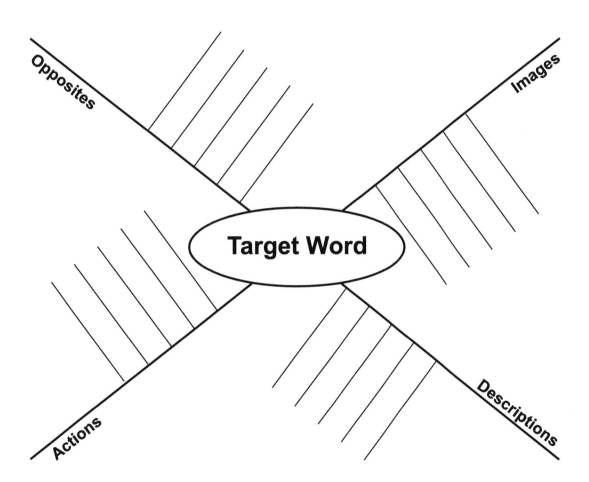

Although you don't have to do all four of the suggested pre-writing activities, don't skimp on the pre-writing stage of the writing process. It is during this stage that writers get the all-important foundations: fluency of ideas, shape, and language.

Formative assessments between stages of the writing process should help the writer move to the next stage.

Showing Knowing

Name: _____   Date: _____

Class: _____

Topic: _____

Explain it	Describe it	Argue for or against it
Draw and label it	Rephrase it	Compare it
Analyze it (take it apart)	Make a list about it	Interview it

Directions: Choose any 2 of these categories and show what you know.

Drafting

Experts in writing instruction emphasize that the drafting stage should feel fluent to the writer, free of worry about the surface errors that will later be corrected. Ideally, students can choose to draft either by pencil or by keyboard.

Formative assessment for the drafting stage may be done by the teacher, writer, peer (critical friend), or a combination, so we'll talk about each separately.

Formative Assessment of the Draft By the Teacher

Remember that your job at this stage is not to proofread and actually correct every surface error. Rather your job is to steer the writer in the right direction and make broad suggestions. Don't feel obliged to comment on every trait.

Use the following structures to organize your feedback to the stuudents as they work through the writing process.

Formative Assessment of a Writer's Draft: Teacher's Guide

Name: _____ Date: _____

Class: _____

Writer_____

Red Light: Stop! These are important points for revision and editing

Yellow Light: Slow down and carefully consider how you can improve

Green Light: You're doing great, keep going

Addressing the Task: You are doing what the question asks you to do.

Red:

Yellow:

Green:

Development: You have sufficient reasons, examples, explanations, facts and figures, details

Red:

Yellow:

Green:

Organization: You have a clear beginning, middle, end. You lead the reader gently from one main idea to the next. You have transitions between paragraphs and within paragraphs.

Red:

Yellow:

Green:

Language: You have used words that are appropriate, interesting, and varied. You have created sentences that are varied and clear.

Red:

Yellow:

Green:

Grammar, Spelling, Punctuation, Capitalization: You have followed the rules.

Red:

Yellow:

Green:

Formative Assessment of the Draft By the Writer

Name: _____ Date: _____

Class: _____

Writer's Guide

What was easy; what I think I'm doing well so far:	What's not so easy; what I think I need help with; what I'm not sure of:

Consider: Addressing the task; development; language; organization; grammar, spelling, punctuation, capitalization

Formative Assessment of the
Draft By Peer (Critical Friend)

Critical Friend's Guide

Writer: _____

Reader: _____

Date:_____

In this draft, which two of the following are strong?

Introduction _____

Examples _____

Reasons _____

Transitions _____

Conclusion _____

Which two of the following need improvement? Make specific suggestions.

Introduction _____

Examples _____

Reasons _____

Transitions _____

Conclusion _____

There's a reason for having different kinds of formative assessment for the teacher, writer, and peer (critical friend): Each of these is tailored to the kind of information that either the teacher, the writer, or the peer (critical friend) is likely to have the skills to provide. Many teachers (myself included) have found to their frustration that peers don't give useful feedback when the field is left wide open, or when they are expected to comment on features of the writing that are, as they say in the military, "above their pay grade." I've had better luck with a more modest array of features, as shown.

Remember that formative assessment is *not supposed to be thorough*. It's just supposed to be helpful enough to allow the student to climb to the next level. Also, the three formats allow for a *variety* of feedback. It's unrealistic to expect that a given piece of writing is going to be reviewed by you, the writer, and a peer. You can switch it up from assignment to assignment.

You may also choose to use all three formative assessments, but only in groups: Teacher takes one-third of the drafts; writers self-evaluate on one-third; peers (critical friends) exchange among the remaining one-third of the class. This rotation allows you to keep the paperwork under control. (Just make sure that you cycle through so that after three assignments, you have done the formative assessment yourself for all of the students, thereby preempting the complaint that you haven't given the same amount of attention to all of your students.

Revision

The formative assessments that intervened in the drafting stage should help the writer shape the draft into a revision. The revision should have substantive improvements, not just (cosmetic) edits. Experienced teachers find to their dismay that what passes for "revision" is simply a rewrite in ink or a type-up on the keyboard. True revision reaches far deeper into the draft. A well-revised piece may have significant differences from the draft.

Formative assessments that get the writer from the revision to the editing phase are those that indicate cosmetic and surface errors. Such imperfections are worth noting because they compromise the relationship between the writer and the reader. By that, I mean that if the reader's experience should be free writer-caused diversions that are, quite simply, a nuisance. It's a nuisance for the reader to have to puzzle over illegible words, stumble over awkward phrasings, fill in the meaning of incomplete sentences and omitted words, and expend an unnecessary amount of energy just figuring out what the writer meant to say because punctuation is either missing or overused. Then there's the matter of the writer's credibility, which is diminished by misspellings, faulty capitalization, improper grammar, and inappropriate language tone.

Please don't think of it as your job to comb through every word of the revision, sharp-shooting for every transgression. Your formative assessment at this stage should be to point out *areas* in need of correction. It is then the writer's job to consult a dictionary, a style guide, or a proofreader. Do not confuse formative assessment with proofreading.

Consider the difference between revising and editing.

The Difference Between Revision and Editing

Revision is about transforming:	Editing is about correcting:

Content: Through the pre-writing and drafting stages, the writer may develop a new conception of where the whole piece wants to go.
 	
Organization: The writer may rearrange sentences or paragraphs. The writer will probably want to add transitions—in and out of paragraphs and from sentence to sentence within paragraphs.
 	
Language: The writer should be upgrading vocabulary to be interesting, varied, and appropriate for the audience. The writer should also be combining sentences, *eliminating redundancy*, and using other rhetorical techniques that make the language more powerful and efficient.
	Grammar:
	  Agreement:
	    Subject–verb
	    Pronoun–antecedent
	    Pronoun case
	    Adjectival
	    Adverbial
	  Usage:
	    Proper verb forms
	    Consistency of verb tense
	  Clarity:
	    Placement of sentence elements
	Spelling
	Capitalization
	Punctuation
	Inadvertently omitted or ineffectively repeated words
	Overall presentation and "look" of the piece

It is very difficult to proofread one's own writing for two reasons: First, if we knew that something was wrong we wouldn't have done it that way originally. The second reason is that our minds play tricks on us, filling in what we *think* is there rather than what is actually in front of us. We do this because we automatically shortcut to make meaning from text. In other words, our eyes play tricks on us. Proofreading is best done by an objective reader, someone well-versed in the conventions of grammar, spelling, punctuation, and capitalization. Granted, the most qualified person in the room is you, but you don't have time to teach, plan, call parents, meet with administrators, serve on committees, differentiate instruction, assess, have a life, and *proofread* everything your students write! So, you and your students are going to have to be content with the proofreading skills of a lesser mortal: perhaps a peer, parent, or sibling would oblige.

To make it easier for this person, I've composed separate guides for grammar, spelling, punctuation, and capitalization. I suggest that these be used as formative assessments, *but not all at once*. Less is more: select one of the four.

Proofreading Guide: Grammar

Properly constructed complete sentences (no fragments, no run-ons or comma splices)	Proper verb form Consistency of verb tense
Subject–verb agreement Pronoun–antecedent agreement Pronoun case agreement	Correct choice of adjective or adverb

Proofreading Guide: Spelling

ie/ei words:	homonyms:
words having suffixes:	words having prefixes:

Proofreading Checklist: Punctuation

Commas	Semicolons and colons
Apostrophes	Quotation marks

Proofreading Checklist: Capitalization

Beginnings of sentences	Places on a map Days on a calendar
Names of people	Words in titles (except prepositions)

As you can see, I've kept these guides *very simple*. For the few students who require a more sophisticated guide, feel free to elevate these. For the spelling guide, for example, you might want to include words ending in *–al* or *–le* such as *practical* and *article*.

Publication

Finally, the workshopped piece is ready to be handed over to an audience of readers. At this point, the reader's purpose would be to absorb the writer's message. The feedback that the reader gives to the writer is formative assessment for the *next* writing piece.

Finished pieces may be made available to readers online (with the writer's name omitted) or on paper as a classroom, grade level, or schoolwide publication. They may be posted on display boards, or simply handed around the room in an open read-around. Authentic out-of-school audiences are available (letters to the editor, letters to elected officials, opinion pieces for local newspapers, writing contests, public blogs).

For student writers to judge and give feedback, they need to be clear on their purpose and intended audience. Here are some guiding questions for the reader:

Feedback Sheet for Published Writing:

Writer: _____

Reader: _____

Date:_____

Am I (as the reader) the intended audience?_____

What do I think is the author's primary purpose? (May choose more than one):

_____ To entertain
_____ To inform
_____ To persuade

Two questions that I would like to ask the author:

1._____?

2._____?

Writing for Assessment

Throughout the process in a writer's workshop, the idea of formative assessment to have it serve as authentic feedback that will help the piece develop to meet the needs of actual readers, not only the teacher. The next kind of writing to be considered in terms of formative assessment is writing for assessment.

The chart below shows the difference between writer's workshop and writing for assessment:

Comparison Between Writer's Workshop and Writing for Assessment

Writer's Workshop	Writing for Assessment (also called "writing on demand" or "timed writing")
Content: The writer chooses the topic and genre.	*Content:* The writer responds to a specific prompt.
Process: The writer attends to each phase of the writing process within a sociable community of writers that is formed by peers.	*Process:* The phases of the writing process are compressed within a time limit. The writer works independently.
Audience: The piece will be offered to various readers.	*Audience:* The piece will be read by the student's teacher or a panel of raters.
Assessment: May be formally or informally assessed.	*Assessment:* Will be formally assessed according to known criteria (rubric or other scoring guide).

Features of writer's workshop and writing for assessment may be combined. You can give students a prompt (specific or general) and have them proceed through the writing process at home and in class, providing some of the formative assessments given above. The goal is to have the students become able to compress the phases of the writing process so that they can meet the time limit that faces them in a test situation.

When I proctored mid-term and final exams, I would observe students hurriedly transcribing their rough drafts onto composition paper. All they were doing was transcribing from pencil to ink, from yellow paper to white. Only surface features were being upgraded: the content remained the same from "rough" to "final" copy. This seemed like inefficient use of exam time.

I developed the practice of requiring that students write a "5-minute plan" rather than a yellow-paper draft. They would receive the prompt and then spend a full 5 minutes creating an outline, or a concept map, or lists, or trial sentences, illustrations, whatever they needed to do to think before writing. Then, I'd encourage them to use the yellow paper, if at all, not to write out the whole essay word for word, as they had been doing, but to just put some meat on the bones of their 5-minute plan before going to the white paper. At the end of the period when the essay was to be completed, I asked for the 5-minute plan to be handed in as well.

Not surprisingly, I found a strong positive relationship between the 5-minute plans and the overall development of the essays. So the 5-minute plan became the focus of my formative assessment for timed writing. When students were shown models of the 5-minute plans of superior essays, they could see how the 5 minutes could best be used to help them think of what to write. The list below shows some ideas for the 5-minute plan:

Five-Minute Plan

- ◆ Outline
- ◆ Word bank
- ◆ Trial sentences
- ◆ Illustrations
- ◆ Labeled diagram
- ◆ Concept map
- ◆ Lists
- ◆ Examples
- ◆ Reasons
- ◆ Venn diagram
- ◆ Tree diagram
- ◆ Q & A: Who? What? When? Where? Why? How?
- ◆ Brainstorm
- ◆ Conversation (if permitted)

In keeping with the belief in "gradual release of responsibility," we might give students the prompt a day or more in advance, encouraging them to mentally prepare. They can come to class with a plan (not a fully completed draft to copy over) on a sheet of paper. Noting which of the students take advantage of this opportunity and which do not is a formative assessment. Eventually, we can reduce the sheet of paper to an index card, ultimately having them able to complete a writing task within a time frame, whether or not they know the prompt in advance.

What Does Excellence Look Like?

What are the goals? What does excellence in writing look like? What are the steps along the way? In Chapter 2, I talked about rubrics for written work. I delineated five categories on the rubric, and I'll remind you of them here:

- *Addressing the Task:* The extent to which the student answered the question to fulfill the needs of the audience.

- *Development:* The extent to which the student provided examples, reasons, anecdotes, illustrations, facts and figures, and other supportive information to fulfill the needs of the audience.

- *Organization:* The extent to which the piece has unity of form; the extent to which the writer leads the reader gently from one idea to the next; the extent to which the piece takes a definite shape so that the audience understands its main ideas and supportive details.

- *Language:* The extent to which the writer has chosen words and composed sentences that are interesting, appropriate, and varied.

- *Conventions:* The extent to which the writer has conformed to the rules of Standard Written English, or to the rules of informal English, should that be the register of language that is expected by the intended audience.

With these criteria in mind, let's have a look at the exact features of each category that distinguishes satisfactory pieces from excellent ones.

Skill Clusters in Developing Writers: Addressing the Task

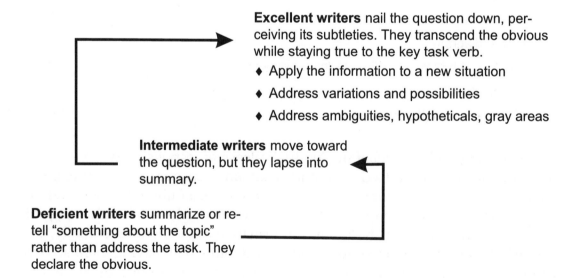

Excellent writers nail the question down, perceiving its subtleties. They transcend the obvious while staying true to the key task verb.
- Apply the information to a new situation
- Address variations and possibilities
- Address ambiguities, hypotheticals, gray areas

Intermediate writers move toward the question, but they lapse into summary.

Deficient writers summarize or retell "something about the topic" rather than address the task. They declare the obvious.

Skill Clusters in Developing Writers: Development

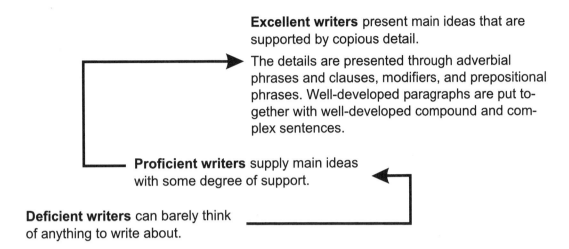

Excellent writers present main ideas that are supported by copious detail.

The details are presented through adverbial phrases and clauses, modifiers, and prepositional phrases. Well-developed paragraphs are put together with well-developed compound and complex sentences.

Proficient writers supply main ideas with some degree of support.

Deficient writers can barely think of anything to write about.

Skill Clusters in Developing Writers: Organization

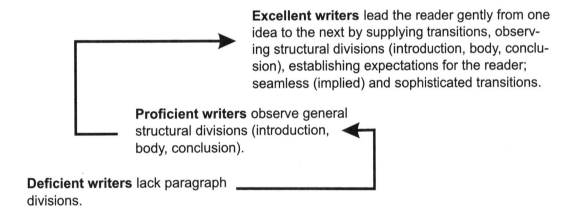

Excellent writers lead the reader gently from one idea to the next by supplying transitions, observing structural divisions (introduction, body, conclusion), establishing expectations for the reader; seamless (implied) and sophisticated transitions.

Proficient writers observe general structural divisions (introduction, body, conclusion).

Deficient writers lack paragraph divisions.

Skill Clusters in Developing Writers: Language Diction and Sentence Complexity

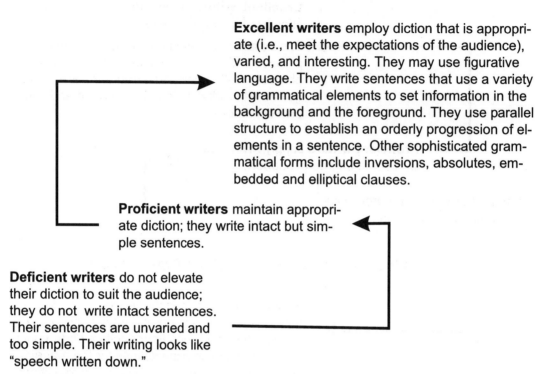

Excellent writers employ diction that is appropriate (i.e., meet the expectations of the audience), varied, and interesting. They may use figurative language. They write sentences that use a variety of grammatical elements to set information in the background and the foreground. They use parallel structure to establish an orderly progression of elements in a sentence. Other sophisticated grammatical forms include inversions, absolutes, embedded and elliptical clauses.

Proficient writers maintain appropriate diction; they write intact but simple sentences.

Deficient writers do not elevate their diction to suit the audience; they do not write intact sentences. Their sentences are unvaried and too simple. Their writing looks like "speech written down."

Skill Clusters in Developing Writers: Grammatical Usage Issues

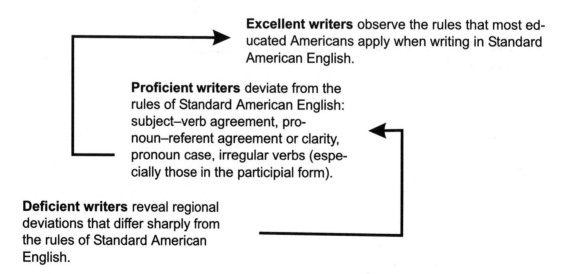

Excellent writers observe the rules that most educated Americans apply when writing in Standard American English.

Proficient writers deviate from the rules of Standard American English: subject–verb agreement, pronoun–referent agreement or clarity, pronoun case, irregular verbs (especially those in the participial form).

Deficient writers reveal regional deviations that differ sharply from the rules of Standard American English.

Deficient writers reveal regional deviations that differ sharply from the rules of Standard American English.

Proficient writers deviate from the rules of Standard American English: subject–verb agreement, pronoun–referent agreement or clarity, pronoun case, irregular verbs (especially those in the participial form).

Excellent writers observe the rules that most educated Americans apply when writing in Standard American English.

Skill Clusters in Developing Writers: Voice and Tone

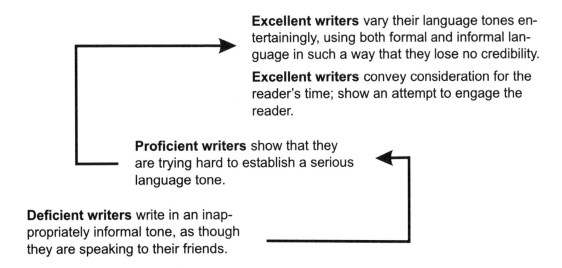

Excellent writers vary their language tones entertainingly, using both formal and informal language in such a way that they lose no credibility.

Excellent writers convey consideration for the reader's time; show an attempt to engage the reader.

Proficient writers show that they are trying hard to establish a serious language tone.

Deficient writers write in an inappropriately informal tone, as though they are speaking to their friends.

Skill Clusters in Developing Writers: Spelling

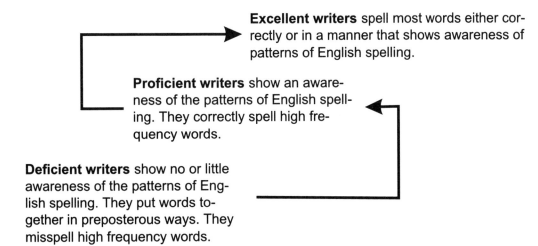

Excellent writers spell most words either correctly or in a manner that shows awareness of patterns of English spelling.

Proficient writers show an awareness of the patterns of English spelling. They correctly spell high frequency words.

Deficient writers show no or little awareness of the patterns of English spelling. They put words together in preposterous ways. They misspell high frequency words.

Skill Clusters in Developing Writers: Punctuation

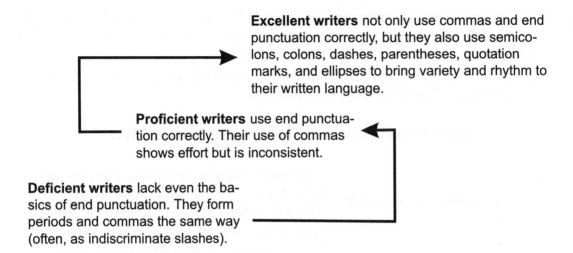

Excellent writers not only use commas and end punctuation correctly, but they also use semicolons, colons, dashes, parentheses, quotation marks, and ellipses to bring variety and rhythm to their written language.

Proficient writers use end punctuation correctly. Their use of commas shows effort but is inconsistent.

Deficient writers lack even the basics of end punctuation. They form periods and commas the same way (often, as indiscriminate slashes).

Skill Clusters in Developing Writers: Capitalization

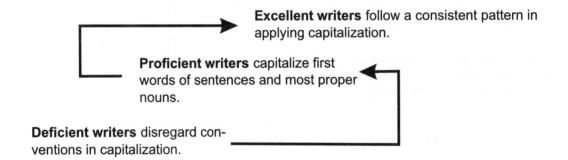

Excellent writers follow a consistent pattern in applying capitalization.

Proficient writers capitalize first words of sentences and most proper nouns.

Deficient writers disregard conventions in capitalization.

Skill Clusters in Developing Writers: Handwriting, Visual Presentation

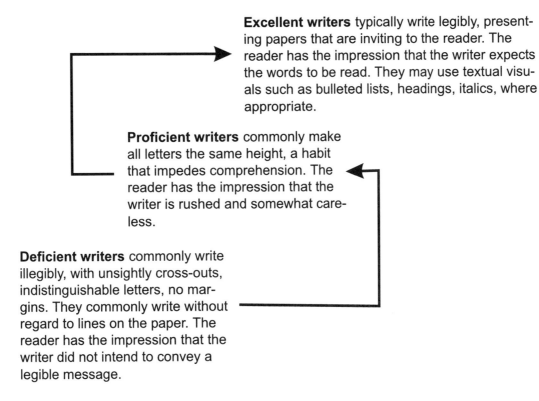

Excellent writers typically write legibly, presenting papers that are inviting to the reader. The reader has the impression that the writer expects the words to be read. They may use textual visuals such as bulleted lists, headings, italics, where appropriate.

Proficient writers commonly make all letters the same height, a habit that impedes comprehension. The reader has the impression that the writer is rushed and somewhat careless.

Deficient writers commonly write illegibly, with unsightly cross-outs, indistinguishable letters, no margins. They commonly write without regard to lines on the paper. The reader has the impression that the writer did not intend to convey a legible message.

Writing to Learn

The third type of writing experience is writing to learn, where the student uses writing as a way to collect, organize, and explore knowledge. When writing to learn, the student is his or her own audience. Writing to learn may take the following forms and serve the following purposes:

- ◆ Reminders
- ◆ Clarifications
- ◆ Organizers
- ◆ Idea collections
- ◆ Attention directors
- ◆ Class notes

I suggest that you encourage students to write to learn, and that you reward their efforts by offering grade-point enhancements to students who show you that they are in the habit of writing for their own benefit. In other words, if they can show you a good notebook that consists of more than just copying from the board, you add points to their quarterly grade or award "homework miles." Writing to learn should be viewed as a valuable assessment, which leads us to the next chapter about note taking.

To summarize, the concept of how formative assessment fits into the writing process is illustrated in the following figure.

**Formative assessments transition the writer
from one stage of the writing process to the next.**

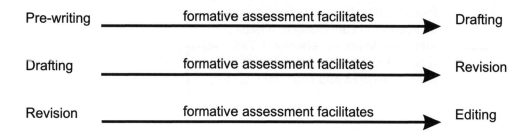

Pre-writing	formative assessment facilitates	Drafting
Drafting	formative assessment facilitates	Revision
Revision	formative assessment facilitates	Editing

6

Note Taking as Formative Assessment

One of the best ways to see whether students understand the flow of information in reading or in class is by having a look at their notes. In *Active Literacy Across the Curriculum*, Heidi Hayes Jacobs (2006) says this about note taking:

> Note taking should be packed with mental action: it involves creative engagement. Interactive note taking provides revealing evidence of authentic student comprehension from both written and aural sources. Interactive note taking replaces the frequent reliance for evaluation of comprehension on *simulated* reading evidence, such as fill-in-the-blank sheets or predetermined multiple choice examinations. Interactive note taking asks (the student) to extract meaning from written, aural, or visual sources and create (his or her) personal and selective reaction. (Jacobs, 41)

Jacobs goes on to assert that note taking is not copying, nor is underlining, highlighting, or hunting down the answers to end-of-chapter questions note taking. "Creative note taking is *extraction* and *reaction*" (Jacobs, 42). Creative note taking involves any of the following higher-level thinking skills:

- Paraphrasing and summarizing
- Organizing, classifying, reorganizing
- Flowcharting
- Establishing a hierarchy of main and subordinate ideas
- Questioning
- Diagramming; graphic representations
- Application and extension

What students need is guided practice with the main formats of note taking. As always, the ELA class becomes Command Central for all things related to language processing. What we are expected to do is to equip students with a toolkit, giving students options and power as independent learners (Jacobs, 45).

Five Note-Taking Formats

- ♦ Outline
- ♦ Chart
- ♦ Extended Map
- ♦ Sentences
- ♦ Cornell Method

Outlining

The outlining method works best for reading and lectures that are highly organized, where the lecture is relatively slow, and process time is provided.

Scenario

Mrs. Kahn, an eighth grade English teacher, wants her students to understand the historical background and social conditions in Victorian England while they are reading *Great Expectations*. She gives the students the skeleton of an outline form that will conform to a 10-minute lecture that she plans to give. Exaggerating the main points, she goes on to describe the penal system, the laboring classes, and the apprenticeship of children as the three main ideas of her brief lecture. After 10 minutes, she will allow a few minutes processing time before asking the students to exchange outlines.

"Keep your outlines," she tells the students. "We'll do this again a few more times while we're reading *Great Expectations*, and you'll see that your outlining skills will improve." Other 10-minute lecture topics will be the life of Charles Dickens, famous characters created by Dickens, and how "the quest theme" operates in *Great Expectations*.

The payoff on the outlines will happen when students find the need to use their notes for the essay on the unit test, which will be on one of these topics.

Charts and Matrices

Notes in the form of a chart or a matrix are appropriate for categorical information that requires classification.

Key words in text whose pattern is classification are these:

- ♦ Kinds of, types of, sorts of
- ♦ Categories, subcategories

- Class
- Divisions
- Provinces, precincts
- Genres
- Characteristics

As her students wend their ways through *Great Expectations*, Mrs. Kahn wants them to use a chart or matrix to keep track of the characters. She gives them this skeletal matrix:

Character Matrix: *Great Expectations*

Character	Motivation (What does the character want or intend to do?)	Relationship to Pip	Object associated with character	Important Quotation

A character matrix is capable of expressing only basic and surface information. It is a scaffolding device that clarifies the plotline. Students use this form of note taking in their social studies, math, and science classes to create a visual of systems and the features of their components. It may be tempting to create a character matrix on the board for the students to copy. But doing so misses the opportunity to have students scan the chapters, either before or after reading, in search of information. Release the responsibility for finding at least some of the information to the students, rather than turning what could be a reading comprehension exercise into a copying exercise.

A variation of the character matrix is the setting matrix in which several environments in the tale (the graveyard, the Gargery home, Miss Havisham's room, etc.) are listed on the vertical axis. On the horizontal axis, you could have headings like "What happened here?"; "Who is there?"; "What objects do we see?"

A chart or matrix is a useful visual cue to understanding various exemplars of a class of things, each having distinguishing characteristics that are displayed clearly on the chart or matrix.

Extended Map

The chart or matrix is capable of holding only surface information across a wide spectrum of information. The extended map is a device that allows the student to go into depth on a single character or place. These are some possibilities:

> Write the "central concept" in the center of the page and draw a circle around it. The central concept to be mapped in *Great Expectations* might be a major character, or a place in which several events happen at different points in the novel, or even a thematic concept such as *education, imagination, destiny, money, social status, separation*. The map is then developed by connecting the central concept to various characters, events, objects, key words, key quotations, historical background, or conflicts. The language on the map should be phrases, not whole sentences. All of the information on the map must be clustered meaningfully and connected with lines and arrows.

The extended map should be developed over time, with the students adding more detail as they read. Mrs. Kahn has the students use a different color with each "session" that they spend working on their extended maps.

Sentences

There are certainly times when you find it appropriate to have students copy from the board. Having them copy from the board can focus the students, reinforce spelling and phrasing, and process information through the tactile modality in addition to seeing and hearing it. To make copying from the board into a creative note-taking activity, you can have students extend their notes into sentences. The sentences can be in outline (indented) or list form.

When students take "sentence" notes, they are strengthening their skills in writing sentences individually (not in the flow of a paragraph). This is important because so many students lose their sense of sentence integrity in the fluency of writing sentences within text (in paragraph form). The "sentence" form of creative note taking forms a strong bridge between writing fragments (phrases) and the ultimate writing goal of being able to compose strong, sturdy sentences within a paragraph.

The Subject–Verb–Object Sentence Pattern

Subject	Verb	Object
Pip	helps	Magwich.
Miss Havisham	exploits	Estella.
Joe	mends	handcuffs.
Pip's conscience	transcends	His society's values.

I like to have students write particular patterns of sentences. The sentence pattern that is capable of containing the most potent information, and that is the most accessible one to students, is the *subject–verb–object* arrangement.

Arranging ideas in subject–verb–object form is a powerful way to zero in on main ideas and key actions. The subject–verb–object pattern allows us to express *who or what did what to whom or what*. If you just leave it open, asking students to write any kind of sentence, you may find that they produce sentences that don't contain a lot of meaning compared to the subject–verb–object pattern.

Grammatically, remember that the direct object answers the questions *Who?* or *What?* to the verb, and that the verb must be an action verb. You miss the power of the subject–verb–object pattern if you mistake a prepositional phrase (which answers *Where?* or *When?*) for a direct object.

As you can see, focusing on the subject–verb–object pattern for "sentence" notes yields other benefits, such as vocabulary development. Students should consciously vary the action verbs that they use. Be prepared to help them generate an inventory of verbs that capture the action of a story, and stress verbs that show influence and change:

- ◆ Influence
- ◆ Transcend
- ◆ Affect
- ◆ Transform
- ◆ Understand
- ◆ Misunderstand
- ◆ Seek
- ◆ Challenge
- ◆ Misleads
- ◆ Deceive
- ◆ Exploit
- ◆ Entice

The bare-bones sentences can then be fleshed out with modifiers (adjectives, adverbs, prepositional phrases) and dependent clauses.

Cornell Method

The Cornell Method of note taking, similar to the K-W-L format, is a three-column structure. In the first column, the student writes questions that she thinks the text will answer. These would be based on an overview of the text, if it is informational text, or on predictions about how the story will unfold, if it is a novel. As the student reads, she jots down *phrases* that answer the questions. Then she lets time elapse before going back to the notes to turn the phrases into complete sentences that answer the questions.

Cornell Method: 3-Column Notes

Questions that I think the text will answer (before reading)	Phrases that lead to the answers to these questions (during reading)	Sentences that can be developed out of the phrases (after reading)

The advantages of Cornell notes are that they allow for focused reading, processing of information over time, and a built-in review and sense-making activity that calls for complete sentences developed from key phrases.

Note Taking for Strategic Teaching

We don't teach note taking as an isolated skill using contrived text. Our teaching of note taking should be folded into our teaching of content (strategic teaching). We are working to create independent learners. The independent learner knows:

♦ *How* to take notes: Give students handouts of the targeted note-taking method, scaffolding by supplying some of the main ideas, having students supply the supportive details.

♦ *What* to take notes on: This requires students to distinguish between main ideas and supportive details. For informational text, the main ideas may be signaled by headings and the organizational structure of the text. Textual visuals, such as charts, graphs, and pictures, direct the reader to the main ideas. Boxed and shaded information often contain supportive or illustrative information, such as anecdotes and case studies that are not in themselves main ideas, but that help us apply the main ideas.

♦ How to *use* the notes: When it comes time to study, just staring at your notes is not active enough to embed learning. Students need to talk over and compare their notes with those of others; reformulate their notes; annotate their notes.

♦ How to *match the format* to the information and its purpose: Deciding on what format of note-taking suits the text is high level thinking (evaluation). They won't know this unless they've had guided experience with the different note-taking genres, matched to different kinds of text.

Assessment of Note Taking: Problems and Possibilities

We should assess a student's notes with a broad brush, using only two criteria: completeness and effectiveness.

The notes are *complete* if they give evidence of continuous engagement in the readings or the lesson. This is not to say that the student has to become a stenographer, recording everything indiscriminately. Complete notes are evidence that the student can tell the difference between main ideas, supportive details, and nice-to-know anecdotes that come up in class.

The notes are *effective* if they accurately reflect targeted concepts, and if they are arranged in a manner that you think the student can understand. Although some students can understand their own notes despite cross-outs, arrows, and other visual distractions, it's a better habit of mind for most students to rewrite their notes neatly, if necessary. Put it this way: If a student can explain her notes to you despite the mess, then the notes serve their purpose; but if she can't explain her own notes, then she needs to rewrite them. Notes are effective when they can be readily located, and when, if the student were to refer to them on a test, or in a discussion, or when doing a task, they would be of use.

I've recommended that formative assessments not be counted toward a student's report card grade; in fact, that is one of the differences between formative and summative assessments. So, I would not recommend evaluating a student's notes for a grade "that counts." I don't think it's necessary for the teacher to look at *everyone*'s notes at the same time, as doing so would be overwhelming. You can collect notebooks from a certain number of students, collect them randomly, and have students self-assess their notes.

The most important reasons for assessing notebooks is to diagnose learning needs of struggling students, and to receive affirmation that your most capable students are picking up your main ideas. Your assessment of a student's notebook can be valuable information for a parent or a special education teacher. With these purposes for assessment in mind, I offer the following very simple rubric for assessing note taking:

Notebook Rubric

Completeness	Your notes show definite gaps in attention what we are learning in class	Your notes indicate that you have been paying careful attention most of the time
Effectiveness	Your notes don't look as though they will be useful to you.	Your notes look as though they will be useful to you in studying for quizzes and tests, completing projects, and participating in class discussion

Because formative assessment should be positive, I recommend that students with satisfactory notes be rewarded. Some rewards might include extra points on tests, erasure of lowest quiz grades, or "homework miles."

"Homework Miles": A Rewards Program for Formative Assessment

Because formative assessments are not supposed to count, especially negatively, on the student's report card grade, we need some other rewards and incentives for the students' efforts. My "Homework Miles" system allows students to accrue a certain amount of "miles" for commendable work on notebooks, graphic organizers, class participation, rough drafts, planning guides, anything that I consider formative assessment. They can cash in their Homework Miles against homework assignments, but only those that are on a list (restrictions and blackout days apply, void where prohibited).

Homework Miles can also be traded in for upgrades, at 10-point intervals, on quizzes. There's actually a hidden bonus here, because, as you can imagine, the act of doing a commendable job on a formative assessment *is also the act of studying* for a quiz, and, at least theoretically, the student would find herself with a higher-than-otherwise grade on the quiz, *plus* the 10-point upgrade.

To keep track of Homework Miles, I give out coupons like the one on the next page.

Homework Miles Coupon

Name: _____ Date: _____

Class: _____

Date of Issue: _____ Date Redeemed _____

For Commendable Performance of _____

Expiration: End of _____ Quarter

Redeemed for:

Free Homework _____ 10 Point Quiz Upgrade: _____

Directions: Congratulations on receiving a *Homework Miles Coupon*. Your coupon may be redeemed for a free homework (restrictions apply) or for a 10-point upgrade on any quiz given during the quarter in which it was issued.

To redeem your coupon, simply fill in the date of redemption and indicate the due date of the *free homework* for which you would like the coupon to apply, or write the title of the quiz to which you would like your 10 points added.

Homework Miles coupons are nontransferrable. Void where prohibited.

Not every single formative assessment receives a reward. While it is true that there is no disincentive (no points taken off quizzes; no zeros or failing grades given for noncompliance with formative assessments), a student's non-compliance or halfheartedness at doing commendable formative assessments *still gives information to the teacher:* What we don't find out about a noncompliant student's academic skills, we do find out about the student's motivation, habits of mind, overall academic outlook based on performance need and deserve recognition and incentives for doing formative assessments to the best of their ability. We want to have a way to reward progress and effort as well as criterion-based performance. Homework Miles allows us to do this without ending up with a report card grade that overstates the student's performance against Standards-based levels. The occasional 10-point boost on a quiz here or there is not going to inflate the student's grade, especially when we consider that the 10 points are the result of commendable work not otherwise recognized in the student's quarterly grade.

Almost every teacher I know thinks that students are overly motivated by numerical grades rather than the internal satisfaction (and self-evaluation) of a job well done to the best of one's ability. While we work out the tensions between the two, Homework Miles offer a way for students to earn grade-point credit for achievements other than those that are recognized on tests.

Summary of the benefits of Homework Miles:

♦ Gives students a sense of choice and control

♦ Is a form of differentiated instruction

♦ Gives information to the teacher about what students know, understand, can do

♦ Answers the question, "What can I do to improve my grade in this class?"

Guidelines for instituting Homework Miles:

♦ Keep it simple: Don't turn your Homework Miles program into an overwhelming paperwork and record-keeping chore.

♦ Don't turn the Homework Miles program into a "busy work" program, giving credit for tasks that are only marginally related to your target learning goals.

♦ Don't allow Homework Miles to replace major assessments or key readings. Don't get into a situation where the student's grade is inflated, rather than equalized, by Homework Miles.

♦ Don't allow Homework Miles to turn into a mad rush to throw papers at you during the last days of the marking period.

- Clarify and post your Homework Miles to your classroom website, making the information accessible to parents.

The time spent teaching, modeling, and rewarding note taking will reap many benefits in academic performance and information processing in all classes.

7

Formative Assessments for Vocabulary Growth

There's a big difference between "teaching vocabulary" and having students actually grow their vocabularies. We "teach vocabulary" in all kinds of ways that *intend* to result in vocabulary growth, but how do we know if they achieve this intended result?

Let's look at the difference between intent and result in vocabulary instruction. The following figure illustrates the features of traditional, teacher-directed vocabulary instruction as compared to instruction that results in actual vocabulary growth.

Does our vocabulary instruction result in vocabulary growth?

(What we may think of as) "Teaching Vocabulary"	(Experiences that are more likely to result in) Actual Vocabulary Growth
The teacher composes the list, based on words that are found in class readings.	The students compose a list of words from the readings that they want to know more about.
The teacher requires the students to look up the words in a dictionary or glossary.	The students make an educated guess about the word as it is used in the context in which they find it. Then, they check their educated guess against a dictionary or glossary definition.
The words on the teacher's word list do not share a strong structural or semantic relationship.	Students are given related words so that they can make connections and learn words in clusters.
Words are treated as individual units of meaning.	Both words and phrases are treated as units of meaning.
The teacher requires that students use the word in a sentence.	The teacher requires that students use the word in a sentence that has substance (at least 12 words), action (contains at least one action verb), and vividness (contains at least one phrase that evokes a clear visual image).
The student's knowledge of the word is assessed based on whether or not the student "gets it right" on a test.	The student's knowledge of the word is assessed based on authentic, contextual use.
The body of words to be assessed is finite and identifiable.	The body of words to be assessed is indefinite, flexible, dependent upon observable growth in the corpus of vocabulary that the student uses in speech and writing.
Assessment criteria are clear, standardized and determined by the teacher.	Assessment criteria are less clear, not standardized, and determined by both teacher and student.
The student learns words in the given form (noun, verb, adjective, adverb).	The student learns the word's morphology (how to transform it into various word classes, aka parts of speech).
The student uses the teacher's exercises to practice use of the word. Such exercises might include fill-in-the-blanks, matching columns, true-false, etc.	The student uses self-selected graphic organizers, such as extended word maps, and charts to practice use of the word.

A Typical Vocabulary Unit of Study

Mrs. Greenfield is a seventh grade English teacher whose students are reading *The Outsiders* as a whole-class reading. She has carefully assembled the following vocabulary list and directions:

> The following is your vocabulary list for *The Outsiders*. Familiarize yourself with the list, and, as you read, note the page or pages on which each word appears.
>
> Look each word up in the dictionary and write its definition. Be sure to include the word's part of speech. If the dictionary gives more than one definition for the word, select the one that matches the context in the book in which the word appears.
>
> Write an original sentence for each word.
>
> You are expected to complete the words for the first half of the book at the end of the first week of our reading. You will be expected to complete the words from the second half of the list at the end of the second week of our reading. You will be tested on these words when we complete the reading of the novel. You will be responsible to know definitions as well as spelling.
>
> Word List:
>
> > Acquitted
> >
> > Aloof
> >
> > Bolt
> >
> > Contempt
> >
> > Credulous
> >
> > Deleterious
> >
> > Dissected
> >
> > Eluded
> >
> > Gallant
> >
> > Impersonally
> >
> > Imploringly
> >
> > Incredulous
> >
> > Indignation
> >
> > Nonchalance

Premonition

Reluctantly

Resignedly

Ruefully

Sullen

Unfathomable

Vaguely

Wistful

At the end of each week, Mrs. Greenfield will "go over" the words by asking volunteers what each word means. She will collect the vocabulary work as homework and deduct two points from the unit test on *The Outsiders* for each word that is "not done" to her specifications (i.e., definitions and original sentence).

The test on all twenty-two vocabulary words will have three parts:

Part 1: Definitions: A 10-item matching column for words and definitions

Part 2: Context: Ten fill-in-the-blank sentences in which only one of the words appropriately makes sense in the context.

Part 3: Spelling: Five word clusters in which one word is misspelled. Students must circle the word that they think is misspelled and write it correctly.

Mrs. Greenfield believes that, following this protocol for all of the literature that the students read as a whole class, she has an effective vocabulary program. She bases her belief in its effectiveness on the fact that students are "held accountable" for a list of useful words in the English language that the students probably don't already know and that appear in the literature that they are reading, making them relevant. Furthermore, she would say that her review of the homework is formative assessment, as it gives her information with instructional implications about the words. She would say that the traditional nature of her protocols for teaching vocabulary as well as having students follow a routine make sense to students and their parents. And, she would cite test results as data to support claims about what students do and do not know about vocabulary.

But Is it Working?

However, Mrs. Greenfield would be the first to admit that she has no evidence that the vocabulary knowledge that she tests for, and gives students credit for, is transferred to their working vocabulary (speech, writing, listening, and reading comprehension). Even when students do recognize a word that was on one of their lists in another contexts, they are likely to point it out as a "vocabulary word" rather than just another word that comprises the English language, as meaningful as any other. Vocabulary words to students, Mrs. Greenfield observes, are in some kind of world apart, a teacher's world, where such words don't fraternize comfortably with the student's natural language.

Mrs. Greenfield notices that students "study" for vocabulary tests by memorizing the word-and-definition unit, and that they have no flexibility with the definition and want to recite the words, along with their definitions, in the same (alphabetical) order) in which the list is given. In other words, they are memorizing a list, not a pattern. They could just as well be learning nonsense words matched to nonsense definitions, for all the meaning the words and definitions have to them. They show no curiosity, no active thinking, no pattern making, no sense of ambiguity about words. They learn nothing about word components, culture and history of language, range or coloration of meaning. Only memorized definitions. Despite the popularity of her approach, Mrs. Greenfield does recognize that something is missing. What is missing is actual growth of vocabulary: use of new words and a strength of the ability to have one new word open doors to others.

If Mrs. Greenfield would be willing to forego the traditional vocabulary instruction described here, if she would accept a paradigm shift into the kind of vocabulary instruction that is less definitive but more durable, she might eschew her teacher-controlled lists. In their place, she would have the students make their own lists. Those lists might be shorter, but the words would be more likely to be remembered and used. As you'll see, Mrs. Greenfield can still give tests at a unit's end, but the tests will call for more authentic word knowledge than the traditional test described above.

Vocabulary Instruction and Formative Assessment for Durable Learning

1. Students select their own words.

Mrs. Greenfield asks the class to thumb through the text that they are about to read. "Let's make a list on the board of words that you want to know more about," she says. (Notice that she does not ask the question in a negative way: "What are some words that you don't know?" Doing that would elicit fewer words as some students would be embarrassed to admit that they "don't know" words, and can mask this by simply offering that there are words that they "want to know more about.") As the students call out words in turn, Mrs. Greenfield pronounces each word and writes it on the board. As she does so, she spells the words aloud and comments briefly on any related words that the students might know: "OK, *indignation*: That's a good one. It's another noun form of *dignity*, as in *self-esteem* or *self-respect*. Can you read the sentence that you found *indignation* in?" The student reads the sentence, and Mrs. Greenfield nods approvingly. If the student misreads the sentence or mispronounces the words, she repeats the correct reading in a clear and casual manner.

Mrs. Greenfield is establishing an introductory level of knowledge about the words: pronunciation, context, word associations. As an added benefit, she's giving the class a preview of the text, which is where the literature lesson meets the vocabulary lesson.

Once the list has approximately 15 to 20 words on the board, Mrs. Greenfield says: "OK, now, this looks like a pretty healthy list for the first half of the book. Now what I want you to do is pick out 10 to 15 words that you'd like to work on this week in your vocabulary journal." She's giving the students choice (therefore, empowerment) in their vocabulary growth. She adds: "If you'd like to include a word that's not up here, go ahead."

2. Students make educated guesses based on word structure and context.

We've all seen students look words up in the dictionary, whether by using a physical or an online dictionary, only to copy the first definition verbatim, without giving any thought to whether that definition makes sense in the targeted context. While there's nothing wrong with using the dictionary for its intended purpose, it's much better to have students consult a dictionary to verify or advance their knowledge about the word, knowledge that comes as a result of intuition about words: use of structural cues (prefixes, roots, combining forms, suffixes), context, and connections. Mrs. Greenfield uses the formative assessment technique of having the students keep a column for "educated guesses." When she checks the vocabulary journal and the "educated guess" column is left blank, filled in with the word's exact meaning, or way off base, she can deduce that the student has difficulty applying intuitive word knowledge to academic vocabulary.

Why would a students leave the "educated guess" column blank, or fake it by writing the dictionary definition verbatim every time, or be completely off base? Let's deal with the first two of these problems together; the third one, separately:

♦ Erika lacks confidence in her ability to make an educated guess. Mrs. Greenfield urges her to just write "something about…" in her "educated guess" column. "Just go ahead and write a very general idea of what you think the word has to do with. You can leave a few blank, but not all of them."

♦ Marni doesn't see the point of making an educated guess about a word that she has to look up anyway. Mrs. Greenfield explains to her (and the class) that the harder we actually think about a word, trying to figure out its meaning, giving ourselves credit for knowing something about words, the more likely it is that we will remember that word.

♦ Gregory's educated guesses are way off the mark, suggesting to Mrs. Greenfield that Gregory needs to work on both structural analysis and context cues. "Start with the beginnings of words," she tells him. "Look for the prefixes that mean 'not,' like 'un,' 'in,' 'dis,' and 'non.'" When you see those at the beginning of a word, and you cover up the prefix and you have a whole word right there looking at you, then you know that the word has something to do with 'not.'" Mrs. Greenfield suggests that Gregory choose words that have 'not' prefixes on the next few lists. This is one advantage of having the students choose their own words.

3. Students then look up the words in the dictionary, selecting and writing the definition that best suits the context.

Mrs. Greenfield instructs the class to provide the number of the dictionary definition that they've chosen as the one most suitable to the context. "The dictionary gives you the definitions with the most common one first, but that doesn't mean that the first definition is the one we're after. Make sure the definition that you select is right for the sentence in *The Outsiders*."

Mrs. Greenfield wants the students to check their educated guesses against the dictionary definitions. If every educated guess is correct, as it is with Elizabeth, then the words are too easy, and Elizabeth is ready to be doing something else more advanced, such as finding synonyms. "Since you seem to be able to figure out all of these words," Mrs. Greenfield says to Elizabeth, "how about if you do morphology charts?" Morphology charts, like the ones on the following pages, show how a word changes its form to be used as a noun, verb, adjective, and adverb.

Morphology Chart

Noun	Verb	Adjective	Adverb
The…	He… *or* They… *or* Must… *or* To…	Which one? What kind? How many? *The ___ truck*	Where? When? Why? To what extent? In what manner?

Here is an example of a Morphology chart which shows the changes of the word "accuse":

Morphology Chart

Noun	Verb	Adjective	Adverb
The...	He... *or* They... *or* Must... *or* To...	Which one? What kind? How many? *The____truck*	Where? When? Why? To what extent? In what man- ner?
accuser accusation accused	accuse accuses accused accusing	accused accusing accusatory	accusingly

4. Students complete their vocabulary journal charts for each word, as shown (see Vocabulary Journal Chart).

As you look at the chart, you'll notice that it requires a variety of cognitive skills and engagements for durable learning. It calls upon intuitive knowledge about language, linking known to new and setting up clusters of like words (patterns), analytical skills, both verbal and nonverbal (drawing or finding the visual), and use of modeling (writing the context). The student's ability to show knowledge in any and all of the components of the chart yields information that both the teacher and the student can use as formative assessment. Such formative assessment is particularly useful if the student is being considered for special education or remedial services.

As formative assessment, Mrs. Greenfield is looking for trends and patterns in the student's Vocabulary Journal Charts: a missing visual here or there for a word that may take some imagination to present visually, blanks left for word components or related words are not noteworthy. But the student who shows a consistent weakness in any of the squares on the chart needs attention because he or she is lacking key skills that are necessary to the all-important ability to strengthen academic vocabulary.

Vocabulary Journal Chart

Name: _____ Date: _____

Class: _____

Target Word: _____

My guess:	Dictionary Definition:	Visual — Draw or find a picture:
	Definition in my own words:	
Complete sentence of at least 12 words: Must have an action verb and a visual.		

Word Games as Formative Assessment for Vocabulary

Word games give you double value: They are formative assessments and a means to practice, expand, apply, and modify language. Word games are a natural way to engage language. They lead to analysis, synthesis, and durable memory of the words and language that we want students to learn.

There is research to support the value of word games in the classroom. In *Building Background Knowledge for Academic Achievement* (2006), Robert Marzano encourages the use of games to stimulate students' vocabulary. To paraphrase Marzano, games

1. Present manageable challenge

2. Arouse curiosity

3. Stimulate engagement because the outcome of a game is uncertain, yet the player feels some sense of control

4. Reform vocabulary learning from the drudgery of drill-and-kill to a meaningful, enjoyable activity that takes advantage of the natural human tendency to want to play with language

5. Foster an appreciation of words and the patterns of language

I would add that word games also provide a means for that all-important social communication with the new vocabulary that students need to make their word-learning durable and engaging. Word games allow for rehearsal of new words, making fragile knowledge (knowledge that won't be remembered and can't be used) into durable knowledge.

When we use word games for formative assessment, we can consider the following features of a student's understanding of the language:

◆ *Speed:* With practice, students should get faster at solving puzzles, executing strategies, and responding to game prompts. If they don't, you should consider either lowering the level, scaffolding by giving them resources or filling in part of the puzzle, or providing explicit instruction in the targeted language area.

◆ *Accuracy:* Analyze the nature of the inaccurate responses: Do they point to a particular language pattern that the student doesn't understand? Use the word games to improve accuracy and reinforce the right pattern.

◆ *Flexibility:* One of the challenges of crossword puzzles is that the solver needs to be very agile when it comes to shifting from traditional (expected) to nontraditional (unexpected) definitions of words, both the words in the answers and those in the clues themselves. Crossword novices need explicit and guided instruction on this flexible way of thinking about words. Also, crossword puzzlers have their own language cues: the clue and the answer must be in the same part of speech; if there's an abbreviation in the clue, then there will be an abbreviation in the answer; if there's a question mark in the clue, then the answer will require some nontraditional thinking. And then there are those obscure words that puzzle makers favor: *epee, tern, essen,* etc. A small crossword dictionary is very helpful.

♦ *Pattern recognition:* Because wordplay involves the gradual recognition of words as they emerge letter by letter, it's very important that solvers come to recognize common letter patterns and reject those that never or seldom appear in English.

Here's a breakdown of the educational value of four kinds of word games:

Word Games and Wordplay as Formative Assessment: Crossword Puzzles

You should know...	How to use for formative assessment
Well-constructed crossword puzzles have a theme. The fact that there is a theme gets students thinking about word clusters for a given topic.	The processes that students use to solve crossword puzzles can give you insight into their ability to think of words flexibly, breaking out of standard definitions and into figurative language.
Students can generate and exchange crossword puzzles by using Puzzlemaker tools (www.puzzlemaker.com).	A student's sense of spelling patterns will also be revealed in a crossword puzzle.

Word Games and Wordplay as Formative Assessment: Jumbles and Anagrams

You should know...	How to use for formative assessment
Although jumbles are not usually themed, you and students can create themed wordlists for the jumble.	Whether a student can or can't unscramble a jumble or anagram gives you insight to their sense of letter patterns and spelling.
Typically, the jumble just mixes up the letters in random order. When the mixed up letters actually form another word, we call the words having the same letters anagrams.	

Word Games and Wordplay as
Formative Assessment: Cryptograms

You should know…	How to use for formative assessment:
A cryptogram is an encoded message—usually a famous quotation or adage—in which one letter stands for another.	A student's ability to work through a cryptogram will give you insight not only into their sense of letter patterns, but also their sense of word patterns in a sentence and their familiarity with famous quotations and adages. You may be surprised at their lack of acquaintance with quotations that you thought everyone knew!
Most solvers begin with single letter words (which have to be the words a or I) and look for common words such as the and that.	

Word Games and Wordplay as
Formative Assessment: Word Searches

You should know…	How to use for formative assessment:
Word searches require figure-ground recognition of words that are camouflaged by random letters.	The lowest level of the word search is the one used most often, i.e., the simple recognition of words among nonwords. To make the activity more challenging, you could provide a definition and have the students hunt for the corresponding word. Still, however, much time is spent looking for words rather than thinking of their meanings. The word search has value for seeing whether students have sight recognition of words. Don't confuse it with an assessment for higher level thinking.

Word Games and Wordplay as
Formative Assessment: Acrostics

You should know...	How to use for formative assessment
In an acrostic, solvers are given a word or phrase that is written vertically on the page. Each letter of this word or phrase then is the first letter of the answer to the clues.	The acrostic will tell you whether students have enough content knowledge to respond to the clues, given the first letter. Because the first letter is supplied, students who can't complete the acrostic have a significant deficit in the targeted content. They will need additional references or further direct instruction.

In addition to these wordplay structures, you might also try the Brain Boosters (http://school.discoveryeducation.com/brainboosters/?pID=brain) on the Puzzlemaker site (www.puzzlemaker.com).

Word Profusions

A word profusion is the result of brainstorming to create a list of words that have something in common. Word profusions can be based on structure (words with prefixes or suffixes, words having a common root, words with a certain number of syllables), or meaning (words about a given topic), or any other commonality that would bring a group of words together. Students create word profusions together, combining their shared knowledge of language into a robust list.

Once the list is created, students can do one or more of the following activities to expand their knowledge and engage in critical thinking as a pre-writing experience.

Five Ways to Use a List of Words as Formative Assessment

1. *Classifying:* Ask students to find some kind of classification system to categorize the words on their list. This activity will be more interesting if groups of students devise their own means of classifying, rather than responding to one that you impose. If each group decides on its own classification system, when the groups report out, everyone will benefit from hearing how other groups decided to arrange their words. The classification that results will cue the organization of a written piece on the topic.

2. *Building:* The goal is to build complex sentences. First, students will create phrases (defined as "part of a sentence"); then, they will build their phrases into simple sentences. Then they will use subordinating conjunctions (common ones are *as, although, after, while, when, until, because, before, if, since*) to turn their simple sentences into subordinate clauses. Then, they will complete the sentence by adding a dependent clause to the subordinate clause, thereby creating a complex sentence.

3. *Breaking down:* Ask students to identify word components on the words on their lists that have prefixes, roots, and suffixes.

4. *Morphing:* Ask students to find words on their lists that can be formed (morphed) into other words by adding a suffix.

5. *Synthesizing:* Ask students to compose a paragraph that uses several of the words on their lists in a meaningful context.

The word profusions and the activities generated from them will give you information about the amount of language that students have and need to express themselves on a topic. The word profusion allows students to bring forth prior knowledge in language that they understand. From there, you can transition them to more elevated vocabulary that corresponds to the vernacular that they know.

Doing the activities further entrenches them in a language-rich experience.

Part III

Performance Tasks

8

Formative Assessment for Performance Tasks

When students work on a multistep project such as a research paper, multigenre presentation, or reading a full-length work of literature, we need to use formative assessments to check their progress. In this chapter, we will look carefully at the many checkpoints along the way of a learning experience that is completed over time. The purpose of these checkpoints is to intervene where we find misunderstandings.

Performance Tasks

A performance task is an assessment that is something other than a test. In English class, a piece of writing that results from the stages of the writing process is the most common performance task. But it could also be a project, a performance, an individual or group report out to the class, or something else. Most performance tasks are multifaceted and take the student more than one day, sometimes several weeks, to complete.

Full-length works—novels, plays, biographies, movies, memoirs—are the mainstay of the high school English curriculum. What we have students do with full-length works contributes to how well they understand, remember, and appreciate literature and apply it to their own lives. Most novels, plays, biographies, movies, and memoirs were intended for private and voluntary indulgence, not as fodder for homework, projects, and tests. That said, what is the purpose of the performance task based on a full-length work? One purpose is assessment, of course, but the process of working through the performance task, if it is well-designed and well-matched to the student, will actually *form and facilitate* learning through the process of doing them. Thus, a well-designed performance task that is well-matched to the student is both the process of learning and its assessment.

What follows are several performance tasks and the points of intervention for formative assessment. The formative assessments at interim points should answer the following questions:

- ◆ Does the student appear to understand the directions for the task?

- ◆ Is the student budgeting his or her time effectively?

- ◆ Does the student need scaffolding or support that other members of the class seem not to require?

- ◆ Is the student making effective use of available resources?

Performance Task I:
Writing a Thematic Paper
Based on a Full Length Work

Product: Literary Essay

In this task, students write a multiparagraph essay showing how one or more full-length works use literary elements to convey a theme.

Directions to the Students

Write a multiparagraph essay in which you show how two full-length works convey the same theme. State your theme in the form of a thesis statement. Develop your essay by making specific references to the literature without lapsing into summary. Refer to literary elements such as plot development, suspense, rising action, climax, denouement, character, relationships, setting, irony, symbolism, tone, structure, point of view, foreshadowing, allusion, genre, figurative language, style, contrast, motif, imagery, and turning point.

Scoring Guide

Addressing the Task: You have drawn two works of literature together by showing how their literary elements express a theme. Your thesis statement enables literary interpretation.

4_____

3_____

2_____

1_____

Development: You have referred to several literary elements, specific examples and quotations from the literature.

4_____

3_____

2_____

1_____

Organization: Your first paragraph consists of a motivator and a thesis statement. Your development paragraphs are supportive of topic sentences that refer to literary elements. You have an appropriate conclusion.

4_____

3_____

2_____

1_____

Word Choice: Your vocabulary is interesting, varied, and appropriate. Your sentences are varied, concise, and clear.

4_____

3_____

2_____

1_____

Conventions: You have observed the rules of spelling, punctuation, capitalization, sentence structure and presentation.

4_____

3_____

2_____

1_____

Checkpoints for Formative Assessment

Checkpoint I: Thesis Statement

If the student doesn't have a well-focused thesis statement, the essay will grow in the wrong direction. The tasks requires the student to find a common theme between two works of literature. Chances are, many students will lean toward books with common plots and then go on to summarize the story lines, never approaching the books on a thematic level.

The teacher, Mrs. Howard, collects index cards on which students have written the following:

Title and Author 1:

Title and Author 2:

Common theme (expresses as a complete sentence):

Thesis statement:

Mrs. Howard requests that this index card be handed in the day after she has given the literary essay assignment (which will be due in its entirety in 4 days). As a result, she certainly knows immediately who has not gotten started. Some of her nonstarters are students who are in danger of failing the quarter, and so she informs parents accordingly by phone or e-mail. She can also judge whether the students have made wise choices in the literature. And she can see the extent to which the students understand how to write a thesis statement that relates two works of literature with a common theme. Based on this information, she may decide to do another whole-class lesson on writing a thesis statement, or she may refer some students to a resource for doing so that is posted on her Website: *http://owl.english.purdue.edu/handouts/general/gl_thesis.html*.

Mrs. Howard takes a quick look at the index cards while the student are doing sustained silent reading. "If I take these home, I might not get to them, and then the kids wouldn't be able to proceed with their essays," she thinks. "They need to get these right back."

Although the thesis statement is the foundation for the essay, at this early point, any thesis statement is tentative because the essay hasn't been written yet. That is to say, the writer's ideas may flower in a direction that requires a narrowing or broadening of the thesis statement. Mrs. Howard wants students to understand how the thesis statement has to serve and focus, not restrict, the writer. So, she has them staple the index card to the final copy. Before collecting papers, she asks the students to talk about if or how their original thesis statement changed as they went through the process.

Checkpoint II: Literary Terminology

During the pre-writing stage, Mrs. Howard had given a specific list of literary vocabulary that she wanted the students to employ in this essay. If they didn't have such a word bank and if they weren't directed to use key literary language, they would probably lapse into summary rather than address the task. The day before the essay is due, she asks the class as a whole to read examples of sentences in which they've used the literary words that she has on the board. Students get ideas from each other, and they are reminded that the final essay is due tomorrow. This classroom activity is formative assessment because it gives Mrs. Howard an idea of how well the students as a whole are understanding the concept of using literary language to develop a thematic essay.

Mrs. Howard has learned from experience that without the formative assessments, fewer students will hand in the essay, and fewer of the essays will have the desired focus and language. Before teaching with formative assessments, she would address the needs only *after* the final copy was handed in and graded, in the hope that students would improve their next essay. But she found that students were much more alert to instruction when it applied to an immediate task in progress, rather than instruction that applied to a completed task.

Performance Task II:
Reader-Response Journals

The Reader-Response Journal, and there are various forms of it, is an excellent genre for formative assessment because it allows students to monitor comprehension as they read, and it shows the teacher what students think is important in the literature. It also gives the students something to refer to as the literature is being discussed in class.

I will describe how the following three versions of the Reader Response Journal can be used as formative assessment:

◆ The Double-Entry Reader-Response Journal

◆ The Cluster and Categorize Journal

◆ The Chapter Keeper

Reader-Response Journal 1:
Double-Entry Reader Response Journal

In this task, students participate in the text by showing what they understand and don't understand as they go along.

Directions to the Students

In a double-entry journal, the reader keeps track of the literal level of the story on the left side, and various responses on the right. The left (literal) side can consist of quotations or notes on story events. The response (right) side can include:

Choose among the following suggestions to develop your double-entry journal. You may choose a variety of these suggestions, or focus all of your responses on one of them.

Sensory Details: As you read, think about how the author engages your five senses. Jot down phrases that evoke images, sounds, sensations, textures, smells, and flavors. Doing this will help the story come alive for you.

Historical Background: If your story takes place in another period of time, do a little research about the time period. Chances are, the author makes reference to historical people and events that you may not know about. You will understand the story better if you increase your background knowledge.

Geographical Background: The story will have more meaning to you if you can clearly picture its setting. You may insert pictures that you find on the Internet of the place(s) in the story. Include both natural and man-made features of the place. Especially, try to find pictures of specific places mentioned in the story.

Predictions and Anticipations: Sharp readers pick up on foreshadowing and clues as to what will happen next in the story. After each chapter, write your prediction about what will happen in the coming chapters *and why.* Doing this will help you pay attention to the events and subtle elements of the story.

Contradictions: Because literature is about real people in real dilemmas, characters don't always keep true to what they say, nor do they always act in their own best interests. Find examples of character's actions that contradict their stated beliefs or that are inconsistent with the rules that they lay down for others. Doing this will help you recognize the irony of human nature.

Reminders: The story may get complicated by introducing several minor characters and places. Keep track of the names of people and places, especially if your book is fairly lengthy and has a lot of characters.

Evocations: What are you reminded of as you read? Literature is supposed to call forth (evoke) your own memories as well as your current life. If something triggers a memory, jot it down and say why. This will help the book have meaning for you and will help you remember it.

Summaries: You may want to write a summary of each chapter *in your own words.* If you do, select quotes for the left side of your Reader-Response Journal that encapsulate important segments of the action.

Points of Confusion: You can use your Reader-Response Journal to talk about what you don't understand as well as what you do understand. Sometimes, keeping track of what you don't understand gathers the information together and helps you to understand it eventually, or at least to ask the right questions.

New Words: Keep track of words that you have never seen before, seen before but never *used,* or words that you are seeing used in a new way. Be sure to include the context on the left side of the Reader-Response Journal. You may look the words up in the dictionary and write the definition, but (1) write your own educated guess about the meaning *before* you look it up, and (2) be sure to choose the definition that suits this context.

Interesting Phrases: One of the joys of literature is the way skilled authors put words together. Create a collection of interesting phrases and then use it as an inventory for your own writing. (If a phrase is no longer than four words, you don't have to cite it.)

Coincidences: Sometimes, stories are based on coincidences such as chance meetings, things that are lost and found, discovery of hidden identities. Keep track of these to help you put the story together.

Key Words and Phrases: Repetition is important in literature. The writer repeats words and phrases to get you to pay extra attention to them. Keep track of these, and then put them together to allow the writer to tell you what he or she wants you to notice most.

Hand-Held Items: Notice any item that a character holds in his or her hand. How is this item used? What is its significance? If you notice hand-held items in the literature, you will be remembering details in the story and relationships between objects and people.

Gatherings: Pay special attention to scenes in which the characters come together for a purpose. Such scenes usually have significance in the story. Think about the tensions that pull the characters apart during the gathering and whether the tensions are secret or out in the open. Notice how the story changes after each gathering. Important gatherings often happen for ritualistic events, such as weddings, near the end of the story. Include the type of gathering, place, characters, mood, and tensions.

Your right side notes should be twice as long as your left side notes. Plan to have approximately *one* page of notes for every *ten pages* of text.

Scoring Guide

Your reader response journal is

Completed

Incomplete_____

Insufficient_____

Your responses indicate

Careful and thoughtful reading_____

Inconsistent care and thought in reading_____

Superficial reading_____

The appearance of your journal can be described as

Neat and legible_____

Inconsistently neat and legible_____

Not neat and not legible_____

The Literary Contract

It might help students to connect to and understand the reading experience if they think of the three-part relationship that exists among the reader, the author, and the teacher.

As the reader, I promise to...

1. give the book at least 50 pages before giving up.

2. read with a serious attitude in a well-lit and quiet place, when I am not tired.

3. not skip anything.

4. picture the pictures, hear the sounds, and feel the textures in my mind.

5. reread confusing parts.

The author promises to:

1. surprise the reader at various points.

2. tie in all elements of the story.

3. respect the reader's intelligence.

4. not write anything worth skipping.

5. write pictures you can picture, sounds you can hear, and textures you can feel.

The teacher promises to:

1. give you enough time to read.

2. answer your (informed) questions

3. tell you the historical background that you need

4. share her enthusiasm for the book.

5. reward your efforts.

Reader-Response Journal 2: Clustering and Categorizing

Another method of reader response is to have students cluster and categorize various elements at certain intervals.

Here's how it works: At intervals in the story (every quarter way through), readers assign a subtitle that embraces the story so far. They then make several categories such as:

Characters: good guys/bad guys

Places: what happens where

Props: hand-held items, who holds them, and their significance in the story

Decisions: what characters have decided what things

Lessons learned: what characters have already learned what things

Mother Nature: how has the weather affected the story so far?

Times of day and night: what happens when

Indoors/Outdoors: what happens indoors? In what rooms? What happens outdoors? Where?

The cluster-and-categorize technique is a way to stop and organize the story. As the class goes over the clusters and categories, students who have lagged the reading will pick up the story. In a perfect world, everyone would keep up with the reading. This not being so, we can hope that "late bloomers" can still catch on.

Reader Response Journal 3: The Chapter Keeper

The "chapter keeper" is another form of reader response. It is more limiting and traditional than the double-entry journal, and so it might appeal to a student who needs a lot of direction and fewer choices.

Directions to the Students: Your "Chapter Keeper" will help you understand and remember the key points of each chapter before your move on. For each chapter, write the following:

1. A one-sentence summary of the chapter.

2. One or two brief questions or observations about the behavior or thinking of the characters.

3. A memorable quotation.

4. A memorable description.

5. A new word: Write the phrase in which it appears, your guess of its definition, the dictionary definition that suits the context.

6. A headline that encapsulates the chapter.

Managing the Paperwork for the Reader-Response Journal

Obviously, you can't expect yourself to read, let alone comment on, all of the journals in their entirety. Here are some sanity-saving suggestions:

1. Have the students keep their journals in a bound notebook, such as the charming black and white "marble notebooks" that are easily available and inexpensive. These are sturdy and compact, easier for you to handle than spiral notebooks or binders.

2. After you collect the journals, roll dice or spin a number wheel to name the page(s) of everyone's journal that you will be reviewing.

3. Stagger your schedule for collecting the journals: You might tell the students to have their journals ready on a given Monday, but you will collect only 20% of them on that day, collecting another 20% as these are returned.

4. Remember that with formative assessment, you are not looking to assign a finite grade. Rather, you are looking to see where students are in their learning, relative to the Standards.

5. To save your sanity, insist that the journal be neat and readable. Encourage students to skip lines and leave a lot of white space on the page.

Beyond the Literary Essay: The 5-Hour Project

Remember that traditional written tasks are only one way for students to express what they know about literature. Here are several formative assessments which call upon a variety of skills and types in intelligence to engage students, individually or in pairs or groups, in complex literature:

Product(s): Various Projects Based on a Full-Length Work

In these learning experiences, students demonstrate their knowledge of literature by doing a nontraditional task requiring imagination and creative thinking.

Directions to the Students: Choose one of the following projects. You may work with a partner or alone. If you work with a partner, you need to submit a Division of Labor Report that specifies exactly who is expected to do what and when. Your project should take you approximately 5 hours (per person) to complete. Please submit a Work Log detailing your hours. Your Work Log should be clear, detailed, and accurate. If your project takes you considerably longer than 5 hours *and* that amount of work is apparent in your project, you will be awarded extra credit. If your project takes you considerably less than 5 hours, then you must make up the hours by either doing all or part of another project, or by elaborating on your project, or by doing two versions of the same project.

1. *Soundtracking:* If this story were a movie, what would the soundtrack be? Make a soundtrack of a story that includes at least 20 cuts, each not more than 10 seconds long. Your soundtrack should have a theme which is reprised at several points. Submit a list of music, with brief explanations of where each piece would fit in, and what kind of mood the music is meant to evoke. Explain how the music creates atmosphere, enhances the action, establishes setting, and gives insight into the characters.

2. *Missing Pages:* In many stories, whole episodes are alluded to, but not developed. What was Madame Defarge's childhood really like? What happened to Heathcliff after he ran off into the storm and before he returned as a gentleman? What did Miss Watson do when she discovered that the slave Jim was gone? Using the language style of the author as much as possible, write the missing pages of a story.

3. *Props Box:* Decorate a shoebox or gift box so that the outside of it represents the atmosphere of a story. Inside, pack articles which, symbolically or literally, represent key points. Be ready to explain the significance of these items to the literary elements.

4. *Dear Mr. Spielberg:* Propose that a particular novel be made into a movie. Refer to the specific scenes that you think would be particularly compelling. Tell what kind of audience you think would be attracted to this film. If the film would play better under a different title, say that that title would be. Suggest actors to play key roles.

5. Make a poster that expresses the essence of the piece. Include the title, author, date of first publication, the first sentence, and the last sentence.

6. Make a map, series of maps, or game board that expresses a character's journey. The map should express both the literal *and* metaphorical journey.

7. Write an illustrated children's book of the piece. You may do an abbreviated version of the whole book, or a particular episode.

8. Write and perform a skit that represents a key episode.

9. Make a tabloid cover that expresses key points in the piece in a sensationalistic way.

10. *Consider numbers:* dates, amounts, times, sums of money, configurations, geometric shapes, schedules, etc. Make a chart that shows the significance of specific numbers in the story.

11. *Consider architecture in the story:* What role is played by architectural features such as front porches, church apses, courthouse steps, jails, stairwells. Make a written or oral presentation that shows the significance of architectural features to the action.

12. Hold a mock trial concerning an incident in the book. Present (orally or in writing) opening and closing arguments by defense and prosecution, jury deliberations, media coverage, evidence.

13. Make a vocabulary guide for a particular chapter. Be sure to show how the words are used in context and where they can be found in the story. Write your definitions so that they sound natural (rather than copied out of the dictionary) and apply to the word as it is used in context.

14. Present the story, or parts of it, as a series of news reports.

15. Make a word collage consisting of key words, phrases, and sentence quotations from the story.

16. Design stage sets for a dramatic version of the story. Design two different kinds of sets. In the first, assume that you have a very large budget; in the second, assume that you have a very small budget. After showing what you would do with each budget, explain which budget was more difficult for you to work with and what you were trying to convey with each.

17. Make costume sketches for various characters. If their dress is explicitly described in the story, include a copy of this description. Explain how the costume gives insight into the inner life, circumstances, and goals of the character.

18. Make a datebook for a character. A datebook consists of appointments, reminders, receipts, phone numbers and little notes stuck inside pockets of the datebook, and other artifacts of a person's daily existence. Use your imagination and be humorous. Present your datebook to the class as an oral report.

19. Write an interior monologue that shows what a character would be thinking at a crucial moment in the story. This can be written as a poem, diary entry, letter to another character, cartoon, stream of consciousness, or any other genre.

20. Write an Introduction and Guide for Reading that could be used by future readers of this story. Include character relationship maps, any terms and historical background that the reader should know, key vocabulary, guides to confusing parts, etc.

21. Make a brochure that advertises the story.

22. Describe how you would set up a literary exhibition for this story if there were such as thing as a literary museum. What would be the centerpiece? What would be the artifacts and captions?

23. Make an author's "yellow notebook." Pretend that you are the author and you are just beginning to gather ideas for this story. Make one or two pages of notes, diagrams, questions, "to do" lists, and crossed-out ideas that show the thinking process that may have gone into writing this story.

24. Show how the Greek and Roman gods play into this story. What Olympian mischief could have been afoot to direct the action and confound the characters? Tell the story as if it were a pagan myth.

25. Using the textual features of magazine writing (pictures, headings, pull-quotes), write an article that is based on this story. Use language that is in the style of a particular magazine.

26. Consider how the writing employs elements of art. What role is played by color? Texture? Line? Give several examples of sentences from various parts of the story which refer to the elements of art: color, line, texture, shape.

27. *Hi, Dr. Phil, thank you for taking my call:* Script a conversation in which a main character seeks professional advice from the popular media figure. To do this, students would have parody the format and mannerisms of the players. The call could be taped and played for the class, including musical interludes.

All of the above tasks can be accompanied by a formal essay and/or oral presentation. Most of these tasks can be done with a humorous twist.

Of course, the specification of 5 hours for this project is arbitrary. The idea is for students to select a nontraditional project that interest them and to keep track of the time it takes to do the work. This task shouldn't degenerate into a race against the clock to complete the task in 5 hours. Part of the learning experience is time management, so you'll need to hear regular progress reports as to how the 5 hours is being spent.

The 5 hours is best spent as a combination of in-class and out-of-class time. Here is a rubric for the 5-hour project.

Scoring Guide: 5-Hour Project

Meaning: Your project reflects an understanding of the task and the story.

4_____

3_____

2_____

1_____

Development: Your project gives sufficient details about the story.

4_____

3_____

2_____

1_____

Process and Preparation: Your Work Reports and Division of Labor Report (if applicable) are clear and well-documented, indicating seriousness about the project.

4_____

3_____

2_____

1_____

Presentation: Your project is neat and attractive, displaying care in presentation. You have observed the conventions of standard English: spelling, punctuation, capitalization, sentence structure (if applicable).

4_____

3_____

2_____

1_____

Summary

In most English classes today, the bulk of the time is spent reading novels, plays, and biographies. Well-constructed performance tasks for formative assessment help students understand and remember complex text *as they are reading*. The assessments shown here are appropriate for assigned reading as well as books of choice.

References

Ainsworth, Barry, and Donald Veigut. *Common Formative Assessments: How to Connect Standards-Based Instruction and Assessment*. Thousand Oaks, CA: Corwyn, 2006.

Black, Paul, Christine Harrison, Clare Lee, Bethan Marshall, and Dylan William. *Assessment for Learning: Putting It Into Practice*. New York: Open University Press, 2003.

C-Test Compared to Cloze Test: http://exchanges.state.gov/forum/vols/vol31/no1/p35.htm

Davies, Anne. *Classroom Connections International*. Courtenay, British Columbia: NCTE. 2004.

Dykstra, Pamela. *An Easy Guide to Writing*. Upper Saddle River, NJ: Prentice Hall. 2006.

Fisher, Douglas, and Nancy Frey. *Checking for Understanding: Formative Assessment Techniques for Your Classroom*. Alexandria, VA: ASCD, 2007.

Jacobs, Heidi Hayes. *Active Literacy Across the Curriculum: Strategies for Reading, Writing, Speaking, and Listening*. Larchmont, NY: Eye On Education, 2006.

Kissner, Emily. *Summarizing, Paraphrasing, and Retelling: Skills for Better Reading, Writing, and Test Taking*. Portsmith, NH: Heinemann, 2006.

Marzano, Robert. *Building Background Knowledge for Academic Achievement: Research on What Works in Schools*. Alexandria, VA: ASCD, 2006.

Nagy, William E. *Teaching Vocabulary to Improve Reading Comprehension*. Urbana, IL: NCTE ERIC Clearinghouse on Reading and Communication Skills, 1998.

North, Sherrin. *Handbook for Differentiated Instruction for Middle and High Schools*. Larchmont, NY: Eye On Education, 2005.

Popham, W.J. "What's Wrong and What's Right with Rubrics." *Educational Leadership* (1997, October): 72–75.

Rowlands, Kathleen Dudden. "Check it Out! Using Checklists to Support Student Learning." *English Journal* (2006): 61–63.

Royer, James M. "Developing Reading and Listening Comprehension Tests Based on Sentence Verification Technique (SVT)." *Journal of Adolescent & Adult Literacy* 45, no. 1 (2001): 30–41.

Zwier, Lawrence J. *Building Academic Vocabulary*. Michigan Series in English for Academic & Professional Purposes. Ann Arbor: University of Michigan, 2002.